D1199438

DOPE

WICKED

Discman

NEW

OMG

FRESH

STYLIN'

NICE

That's

SO 90s!

**A POP-CULTURAL GUIDE
TO THE RADDEST DECADE**

That's SO 90s!

BY JO STEWART

ILLUSTRATIONS BY LISA GILLARD

Smith Street Books

CONTENTS

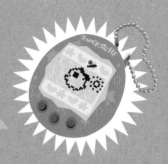

INTRODUCTION

Load some batteries into your Discman, slip into a pair of Doc Martens boots, and spray on some White Musk perfume from The Body Shop, you're now entering the matrix of 90s nostalgia.

An extraordinary decade bursting with pop cultural goodness, the 90s was quite the time to be alive (before people starting saying 'what a time to be alive').

The Golden Age before social media came along and ruined our concentration spans, the 90s had our full attention. Whether it was being glued to the couch while watching *Friends*, lying on your bed listening to Pearl Jam's *Vitalogy* from beginning to end, or having the time of your life at Lollapalooza without taking a single selfie, the 90s enabled full immersion in whatever you were experiencing.

Grunge, Britpop, boy bands and hip-hop dominated the charts, court cases became legitimate entertainment and ground-breaking sitcoms rewrote the rules of television. Your local video store was still the place to be on a Saturday night and the best way to meet people wasn't on an app but by striking up a conversation with a stranger in a bar.

If you wanted to be cool in the 90s, climbing the ladder at a big corporation was social poison. Multinational brands were evil and selling out was for suit-wearing yuppies with car phones. For Generation X, being a slacker was iconic, and aspiring to own a company by the time you were twenty-five was just gross.

One of the hardest things about writing a book dedicated to an era jam-packed with cultural touchstones is deciding what to include and what to leave out. Is *Full House* more 80s than 90s? Would dedicating three paragraphs to Michael Bolton's hair be overkill?

You'll find that some aspects highlighted in this book didn't originate in the 90s, but if it rose to prominence or made a big impact anytime between 1990 and 1999, then it belongs in this book, even if it was invented or created in the 80s or before.

While it's impossible to do such a glorious decade justice in just one book, I've given it a shot. Whether you were lucky enough to live it the first time around or are wistful for a decade you never got to experience, I hope you enjoy this illustrated love letter to a decade that gave us so much.

MOVIES

The era before digital downloads replaced the cinema experience, crowds flocked to movie theatres to see the latest, must-see films. In the 90s, big budget blockbusters smashed box office records, erotic thrillers with twisted plotlines had a moment, grunge musicians moonlit in feature films and adults discovered that full-length animated movies weren't just for kids. As a decade that produced some of the greatest movie soundtracks of all time, 90s movies are still music to our ears.

PRETTY WOMAN

The start of a new decade brought Hollywood box office gold when Garry Marshall's *Pretty Woman* was released in March 1990. The unlikely pairing of Richard Gere (playing multimillionaire powerbroker Edward Lewis) and Julia Roberts (playing down-on-her-luck sex worker Vivian Ward) proved to be a winning combination, with the movie earning Julia Roberts a Golden Globe Award win.

Despite receiving mixed reviews from critics, the film grossed more than US$450 million worldwide, earning back its production costs within one weekend of its release. The killer soundtrack went triple platinum thanks to a robust line-up of genuine bangers including a power ballad from Roxette, a throwback belter from Roy Orbison, a one-hit wonder from Go West and Prince's 'Kiss' (famously sung by a Walkman-wearing Vivian in a bubble-filled tub).

Pretty Woman's modern fairy tale is an all-out festival of early-90s excess. Product placement of a sleek Lotus Esprit ensured a triple-fold increase in Lotus sales in the US. The film put Rodeo Drive on the map and is packed full of iconic fashion moments like Vivian's unforgettable brown, polka dot dress. The timeless appeal of *Pretty Woman* – and Julia Roberts' dazzling smile – ensures it's an enduring guilty pleasure decades after its debut.

90s CROSSOVER ALERT!

Look out for Jason Alexander playing a lecherous creep before he rose to fame as hapless George Costanza in *Seinfeld*.

SLEEPLESS

in Seattle

Rom-com wizard Nora Ephron's 1993 romance turns the schmaltz dial up to eleven, revelling in sentimentality while tipping its hat to the greats of the genre. Sure, snobbish critics delight in pointing out this endearing film's apparent flaws, but its unashamed sincerity ensures it will be watched and re-watched by fans of rom-coms for decades to come.

Centring on the lives of Seattle-based architect Sam Baldwin (Tom Hanks) and Baltimore-based reporter Annie Reed (Meg Ryan, at the height of her total domination of the genre), *Sleepless in Seattle* catalogues their preposterous journey to finding true love. After hearing widower and single dad Sam on a late-night radio talk show, starry-eyed Annie (despite being engaged to another) embarks on a wild-goose chase (bordering on low-level stalking) to connect with the man she's drawn to.

With a stellar supporting cast including Bill Pullman, Rosie O'Donnell, Tom Hank's real-life wife Rita Wilson – and two of the most adorable child actors to ever grace the screen (Ross Malinger and Gaby Hoffmann) – *Sleepless in Seattle*'s other notable star is the city of Seattle itself. From Sam's iconic floating house, to the longstanding Athenian Inn and iconic Pike Place Market, this film is not only a tribute to true love but also a love letter to its titular city.

A stardust-sprinkled soundtrack filled with old-school romantic standards by Nat King Cole and Jimmy Durante, combined with on-screen references to classic 1957 romance film *An Affair to Remember* makes *Sleepless in Seattle* a starry-eyed nostalgia-fest befitting of annual Valentine's Day television re-runs.

90s CROSSOVER ALERT!

This film makes reference to Al Yeganeh, the real life 'Soup Nazi' who *Seinfeld* dedicated a whole episode to two years later.

FORREST GUMP

In 1994, Steven Spielberg followed his dinosaur epic *Jurassic Park* with a decades-spanning, hero's journey tale about a simple man named Forrest Gump, who naively manages to outperform every other human being on earth with his amazing feats and incredible achievements. *Forrest Gump* could be described as a love letter to modern American history, a masterful meditation on life itself or a fantastical popcorn movie, depending on who you talk to.

While some critics viewed the film as overly sentimental sickly sweet Hollywood confection, moviegoers and The Academy of Motion Picture Arts and Sciences completely fell for the movie's charms. *Forrest Gump* went on to become America's highest grossing film of 1994 and win a stack of Academy Awards including Best Picture, Best Director and Best Actor (gifting Tom Hanks rare back-to-back Best Actor Oscars following his win for *Philadelphia* the previous year).

The hugely successful double-disc soundtrack of American classics was snapped up by more than 10 million fans. Featuring a killer pop line-up mostly from the 60s and 70s – including hits from Bob Dylan, Aretha Franklin, The Beach Boys and Buffalo Springfield – served as a potent reminder of just how damn good music from that era was.

Today, *Forrest Gump* maintains immeasurable pop-culture cache. Singer–songwriter Frank Ocean wrote a track about Forrest, and the Bubba Gump Shrimp Company, a restaurant chain inspired by the movie, has more than forty-five locations around the world. People still dress as Forrest to compete in marathons and in 2018 a British man named Rob Pope replicated Forrest's epic run around the United States. Monument Valley's Forrest Gump Point is still visited by fans keen to see the place where scenes from the movie were shot.

As the man who served in the Vietnam War, became a professional table tennis player, met several US presidents, taught Elvis Presley to dance and ate chocolates on a park bench, Forrest Gump is still an instantly recognisable icon of the silver screen. Like him or loathe him, Forrest Gump is here to stay.

GROUNDHOG DAY

In 1993, Bill Murray and Andie MacDowell unexpectedly stole audiences' hearts in Harold Ramis's peculiar, fantasy/romance/comedy/drama.

In one of his most famous roles, Bill Murray is selfish, cynical TV weatherman Phil Connors, who is sent to the small town of Punxsutawney, Pennsylvania to cover an annual ceremony involving a psychic groundhog known to prophesise the coming of spring. Connors finds himself inexplicably trapped in an endless loop, reliving the same shitty day again and again and again, waking every morning at 6 am to the aggravatingly cheerful sounds of Sonny and Cher's 'I Got You Babe' blasting out of his clock radio. As his character runs the full gamut of his emotional and philosophical journey Bill Murray is able to convey the full range of human expression as he steps in that same puddle and meets the very irritating Ned Ryerson each morning.

Such is the pervasiveness of this American classic, decades later the term 'Groundhog Day' is still used to describe a familiar, recurring situation or scenario they'd prefer not to be experiencing, such as, yet another boring as hell day at work. And so strong is the love for this film, a Broadway musical spin-off premiered in 2017, twenty-four years after the movie's initial release.

Years later, fans still debate the deeper meanings of the film, still shudder when they hear 'I Got You Babe' on the radio and still get down on their knees and thank the movie gods that John Travolta wasn't awarded the part of Phil the weatherman (yes, he was considered for the iconic role).

90s TRIVIA ALERT!

Bill Murray was bitten several times by the various groundhogs used to play Punxsutawney Phil, with a rabies shot required to get him through the filming process.

THE SIXTH SENSE

Pulling off one of the greatest plot twists in cinematic history, *The Sixth Sense* was one of the most talked about films of the late 90s. Grossing more than US$670 million worldwide, audiences around the globe flocked to theatres after word got out that this sleeper hit was the must-see movie of the American summer.

Following the experiences of a fragile boy who communicates with spirits (played brilliantly by Haley Joel Osment), his worried mother (Toni Collette) and the child psychologist (Bruce Willis) tasked with trying to help him, *The Sixth Sense* is an absorbing supernatural thriller that quietly grabs viewers by the throat and doesn't let go until the big twist is revealed at the end.

Nominated for six Oscars, four BAFTAs and two Golden Globes, *The Sixth Sense* reinvigorated the horror thriller genre (and reinforced the very real need for spoiler alerts). Considered M. Night Shyamalan's greatest work, nothing the writer and director has produced since has had an impact quite like *The Sixth Sense*.

Perhaps the film's most enduring legacy is the oft-quoted 'I see dead people' catchphrase. Parodied and referenced by films, talk shows and television series ever since, variations of the notable line have been repeated in *Scary Movie*, *Bad Boys II* and in shows as varied as *The Simpsons*, *Six Feet Under*, *Gilmore Girls*, *Hannah Montana*, *South Park*, *Family Guy*, *Entourage* and *Absolutely Fabulous*. Just like many of the tortured spirits depicted in the film, the popular phrase is a line that just won't die.

90s TREND ALERT!

Hollywood was on a major roll with epic plots twists in the 90s, with the decade spawning many memorable movies with surprise endings, including *The Usual Suspects*, *The Crying Game*, *Primal Fear* and *Fight Club*.

HOME ALONE

Considered one of the greatest holiday movies ever made, *Home Alone* debuted in cinemas in late 1990 and has been a solid fan favourite ever since.

Penned by screenwriting legend John Hughes, *Home Alone* is the story of an eight-year-old boy called Kevin (played by the biggest child actor of the 90s, Macaulay Culkin) who is left home alone in Chicago for Christmas after a parenting fail. *Home Alone* had many kids pondering what they would do if they had the power to make their family disappear.

Viewers follow Kevin as he recovers from the panic of being left behind by his large family to enjoy the fringe benefits of being free from parental control (namely: slapping on aftershave and eating massive bowls of ice cream while watching rubbish TV).

Things take a turn for the worse when a pair of bumbling burglars (Joe Pesci and Daniel Stern) try to break in. Plucky Kevin manages to evade, elude and brutally assault the intruders by devising a series of elaborate traps, while his frantic mother desperately tries to get back to him (with the help of Gus Polinski, the Polka King of the Midwest, played by John Candy).

Traversing territory from slapstick comedy to touching family drama, it's a tad perplexing that a comedy about parental neglect (and, arguably, a child psychopath) could become the year's highest grossing film and a bona fide Christmas movie classic. *Home Alone* is one of those movies where you just have to suspend your connection to reality for a while to enjoy the ride.

90s TRIVIA ALERT!

It's not exactly breaking news that Macaulay Culkin bears the emotional scars of a childhood spent in front of the camera, but *Home Alone* left him with an actual physical scar, caused by Joe Pesci biting his finger during a scene.

TOY STORY

It's hard to imagine life without Pixar films, but before 1995 there were none. And then *Toy Story* hit screens and changed the film world forever. As the very first computer-animated feature-length film to grace our screens, the hype surrounding Pixar even before *Toy Story*'s release was considerable.

While *Toy Story* could have ended up as little more than a gimmick showcasing flashy new technology, the film's endearing themes, wholesome storyline, witty script (penned by Joss Whedon) and big name cast featuring Tom Hanks and Tim Allen, ensured its success.

Consistently rated as one of the best animated films of all time, *Toy Story* is a buddy movie that gives life to inanimate toys. The film's unusual emotional depth – a quality that would become the Pixar hallmark – resonated with children and adults alike, which translated to wild critical acclaim and box office success.

Perfectly suited to merchandise sales, Woody, Mr Potato Head and Buzz Lightyear toys can still be found in children's bedrooms today (where they presumably come to life whenever we're not around).

Nominated for Oscars, Golden Globes and more, *Toy Story* is a true 90s hit and its popularity continues to stretch well beyond the decade, spawning several acclaimed sequels, video games, theme park rides and countless Halloween costumes.

Paving the way for Pixar's many other successful animated films (including *Monsters Inc.*, *The Incredibles*, *Up*, *Finding Nemo*, *Ratatouille*, *Inside Out* and *Cars*), *Toy Story*'s legacy is profound and isn't over yet, with *Toy Story 4* hitting screens in 2019.

Just like its hero Buzz Lightyear, the *Toy Story* franchise continues to go to infinity and beyond!

THAT'S SO 90S!

The family flick

The 90s were a great decade for family entertainment. Witches were in again thanks to *Hocus Pocus* and the still-terrifying adaption of Roald Dahl's *The Witches*. The special connection between children and animals was highlighted in *Free Willy* and *Beethoven*, while the star power of Michael Jordan ensured *Space Jam* was a hit. People who grew up in the 90s still have a soft spot for *The Mighty Ducks*, still cry in *My Girl*, will sing along to *The Lion King* and dearly wish that a possessed board game like *Jumanji* existed in real life.

MRS DOUBTFIRE

Despite essentially promoting the morally questionable antics of an unhinged parent who dupes and deceives his own family in order to become closer to them, the 1993 family comedy–drama *Mrs Doubtfire* is still a beloved fan favourite. Co-starring Sally Field and Pierce Brosnan, the film is undoubtedly carried by the comedic genius of screen legend Robin Williams who won a Golden Globe for his memorable performance.

As the plot goes, following a separation from his wife and desperate to spend more time with his kids, Williams' Daniel Hillard transforms himself into Scottish nanny Euphegenia Doubtfire in order to insert himself in the family home and win back his family's trust.

While *Mrs Doubtfire* can be read as problematic in a number of ways by today's standards, in 1993 it was a massive hit as the second highest grossing film of the year (coming in behind *Jurassic Park*) and one of the most talked about movies of the decade.

There is no doubt, however, about the brilliance of Williams' performance. Throw in the fantastic San Francisco location and you've got a highly entertaining vehicle for Robin Williams to show off his comedy prowess, a rarefied talent that is very much missed by film fans around the globe.

INDEPENDENCE DAY

A guilty pleasure sci-fi blockbuster that propelled Will Smith straight onto the Hollywood A List, *Independence Day* blasted its way into the record books by becoming the highest grossing film of 1996.

An overblown, action-packed hit directed by the overlord of the global disaster genre Roland Emmerich, *Independence Day* is an exercise in pure 90s schlock. Starring Will Smith, Bill Pullman and Jeff Goldblum and jazz-pianist-turned-actor Harry Connick Jr., the film was released over the Independence Day holiday weekend in America – a genius marketing move that paid off handsomely with the film posting the biggest opening weekend of the year.

Let's face it, *Independence Day* manages to get away with some seriously silly shit, all in the name of defending planet Earth from an alien invasion. Extra-terrestrials get punched in the face, a heroic canine jumps through a ball of flames to safety, the President of the United States flies a fighter jet into combat and the White House gets blown to smithereens. But what else would you expect from a script written in a mere four weeks?

While loaded with stereotypes, the well-paced film is a glorious, over-the-top, jingoistic piece of pure escapism, filled with explosions, cheesy dialogue and a predictable outcome (spoiler alert: many alien asses get kicked).

Reported to have earned more than US$817 million worldwide, *Independence Day* revived the disaster-movie genre and also proved that a black actor could not only lead an action blockbuster, but break box office records in the process. Will Smith would go on to co-star with aliens again in *Men in Black*, released the following year.

While the Alien and Predator film franchises continue to be revived with some success, when an *Independence Day* sequel was released in 2016, it failed to recapture the magic of the original, proving that this type of movie is a unique product of the 90s and is best left there (along with Harry Connick Jr.'s acting career).

JURASSIC PARK

In one of the world's most successful page-to-screen adaptations, when placed in the hands of director Steven Spielberg, Michael Crichton's science-fiction page-turner morphed into a genuine, worldwide phenomenon.

Starring Sam Neill, Laura Dern and Jeff Goldblum (with an honourable mention to Wayne Knight, aka Newman from *Seinfeld*), *Jurassic Park* cost US$63 million to make but grossed a whopping one billion bucks. Audiences around the world lapped up the outlandish story of what happens when scientists play God and clone extinct species of highly dangerous, volatile, hungry dinosaurs to populate an amusement park. What could possibly go wrong?

Spielberg's highly ambitious vision required revolutionary work from the visual effects artists at George Lucas's Industrial Light & Magic, and the movie's awe-inspiring combination of animatronics and CGI still stands up today (the movie is a very good argument for the enduring quality of practical effects over digital).

Aside from the visual splendour of the dinosaurs, *Jurassic Park* also gave us the indelible image of Jeff Goldblum's sexily bare-chested Dr Ian Malcolm reclining in a pose that has inspired countless memes, a Funko action figure and a giant (slightly creepy) statue that was erected in front of London's Tower Bridge to celebrate the film's twenty-fifth anniversary.

The 1993 premiere (attended by none other than 90s power goddess Princess Diana) was just the beginning of *Jurassic Park*'s dream run. Spawning sequels and a current-day reboot, merchandise, an animated series, Jurassic Park: The Ride at Universal Studios (designed by Spielberg himself) and a McDonald's value meal, the film has all of the elements of a commercial juggernaut, but its enduring influence and popularity really comes down to just how damn entertaining it is.

90s CROSSOVER ALERT!

Jurassic Park's notoriously tense T-Rex scene is spoofed in 90s bro-comedy *Wayne's World 2*.

CLUELESS

High-charm 90s talents Alicia Silverstone, Brittany Murphy and the ageless Paul Rudd unite in this landmark coming-of-age flick that proves that popular teen movies can reach greatness.

Debuting in 1995, *Clueless* was written and directed by Amy Heckerling and loosely based on Jane Austen's *Emma*. Centring on the match-making exploits of wealthy, superficial but well-meaning Cher Horowitz (played by Alicia Silverstone, fresh from appearing in a trilogy of Aerosmith film clips), the film's sharp writing, insanely quotable dialogue and self-aware characters made it a classic of the teen-movie genre.

But the real star of *Clueless* is the clothes. Rich-kid Cher's enviable wardrobe was filled with 90s favourites Calvin Klein, Jean Paul Gaultier and Azzedine Alaïa, and *Clueless* ushered in a generation of brightly coloured preppy styles that are as synonymous with 90s fashion as the flannelette shirt: headbands, knee-high socks, berets, tartan suits, oversized blazers and plaid miniskirts.

A relentlessly positive movie filled with bright colours and upbeat tunes, *Clueless* offers an alternative view of the 90s that is delightfully at odds with the lazy slacker vibe and disaffected grunge scene put forward in other films of the decade.

Yes, spoilt, privileged, sheltered Cher is absolutely clueless about the realities of the world, but as a high schooler who lives in Beverly Hills and has a digital, rotating wardrobe, what would you expect? Don't like *Clueless*? Whatever!

ROMEO + JULIET

Baz Luhrmann's 1996 reboot of Shakespeare's tale of doomed teenage love managed to merge gun violence and gang warfare with heartfelt monologues on the nature of love. Throw in some next-level fancy-dress costumes and a kicking soundtrack full of catchy 90s tunes and you've got yourself a party.

An audacious, creative film geared towards the MTV Generation, *Romeo + Juliet* starred Claire Danes and a baby-faced Leonardo Di Caprio as the titular star-crossed lovers from warring families, with Paul Rudd also making an appearance as Paris.

Filmed in Mexico and California, the stylised violence, rapid-fire editing and overblown score attracted everything from hyperbolic praise to sheer revulsion from film critics. But else what could be expected of a Shakespeare adaptation that takes its cues from Spaghetti Westerns?

The soundtrack is just as iconic as the film and is often heralded as one of the greatest of the 90s. In fact, the album was so popular it posted triple platinum sales in the US and quintuple platinum sales in Australia.

Featuring huge 90s artists such as Garbage, Everclear and Radiohead, the soundtrack brims with the optimism and purity of young love. Standout soundtrack moments include the endearing 'You and Me Song' by The Wannadies and Des'ree's heart-tugging 'Kissing You' (the perfect accompaniment to seeing Leonardo and Claire lock eyes through a fish tank).

Baz Luhrmann went on to direct *Moulin Rouge!* (the final film in his 'Red Curtain Trilogy', following *Strictly Ballroom* and *Romeo + Juliet*), *Australia* and *The Great Gatsby*, but for many viewers, *Romeo + Juliet* remains their number one crush.

TITANIC

Let's cut to the chase: there was definitely enough room for Jack and Rose on that wooden door plank.

Now that that's settled, *Titanic* wasn't just *the* hit movie of 1997, it was a worldwide sensation that toppled records, dominated awards ceremonies and made audiences cry rivers of salty tears.

Starring dream team and real-life BFFs Leonardo DiCaprio and Kate Winslet as well as Billy Zane and Bill Paxton, *Titanic* took the disaster-movie format, gave it a melodramatic overhaul and supercharged it with a bombastic Celine Dion power ballad.

Audiences fell in love with Jack and Rose, hated on Cal Hockley the unmanly lifeboat spot–stealer, and wondered if they'd ever be as old as Gloria Stuart (who was nominated for an Oscar for her turn as Old Rose).

Grossing more than US$2 billion, *Titanic* is the second highest grossing film of all time (James Cameron holds the number one position with *Avatar*) – but it all could have gone horribly wrong. Madonna was considered for the role of Rose, Enya was originally approached to compose the score and during filming, fifty members of the cast (including Bill Paxton) were sent to hospital after eating chowder that had been laced with the potent drug Angel Dust.

Love it or loathe it, there are few film songs as iconic as Celine Dion's 'My Heart Will Go On', which won an Oscar for Best Original Song (one of the eleven Oscars the film claimed that year) and became one of the best-selling singles of all time. Today, it's hard to separate the popularity of the film with that of the song that became an instant wedding and funeral favourite.

Apart from its remarkable record-breaking box office run, *Titanic*'s influence is still very present in our lives. 'My Heart Will Go On' still gets regular airplay on adult-contemporary radio stations, and the film got another run in cinemas to celebrate its twentieth anniversary. And you just try getting on a boat and not re-enacting Jack and Rose's famous 'I'm flying' scene.

THE CRAFT

Don't believe the lukewarm reviews from critics and poor ratings found on review sites, with its winning exploration of female relationships and empowerment – with a little witchcraft thrown into the mix – The Craft was hot property with teen girls in the 90s.

Part high school movie, part cautionary tale, part supernatural horror, 1996's The Craft made the occult cool again. Following the lives of Nancy (Fairuza Balk), Bonnie (Neve Campbell), Sarah (Robin Tunney) and Rochelle (Rachel True), the film covers the usual teen-movie territory – bullying, jealousy, love triangles, social cliques, body hang-ups – but spices things up with rituals, magic spells, bugs, snakes, candles, crystals and lots of heavy eye makeup.

The movie's appealing witchy girl-power themes prompted a wave of teens to start reading up on Wicca in libraries, holding slumber party séances and chanting the words, 'light as a feather, stiff as a board', over and over again, desperately attempting to levitate just like Rochelle did in the film.

Watching the film now is an exercise in hardcore 90s nostalgia: the soundtrack is a hit parade of artists at their peak (including Juliana Hatfield, Elastica, Spacehog and Jewel) and the fashion is onehundred per cent pure 90s gold (think tartan miniskirts, chokers and chunky leather boots).

Before The Chilling Adventures of Sabrina, Salem and American Horror Story, there was The Craft and it was magic.

90s CROSSOVER ALERT!

The Love Spit Love cover of The Smiths' 'How Soon Is Now?' plays in The Craft. It obviously has pretty spooky vibes as it was later used as the theme song for the witchy TV classic Charmed.

CRUEL INTENTIONS

Towards the end of the 90s, teen movies took a rather vicious turn, with *Cruel Intentions* throwing out the rulebook with a twisted plot filled with blackmail, teen sex, bullying, drugs, frenemies and a sort-of incestuous relationship between a step-brother and step-sister.

Starring Reese Witherspoon, Ryan Phillippe, Sarah Michelle Gellar, Selma Blair and a regrettably peroxide-blonde Joshua Jackson, *Cruel Intentions* is a film full of mean teens getting up to no good. Released in 1999, the film soon became a hit with teens who loved the risqué scenes, hot cast and perverse ideas *Cruel Intentions* introduced to viewers hungry for something beyond the usual vanilla teen flick fare.

The story was loosely based on *Les Liaisons dangereuses*, a book about the French aristocracy published in the 1700s, most famously adapted in 1988 as the film *Dangerous Liaisons* starring Glenn Close, John Malkovich and Michelle Pfeiffer. Where that film earned seven Oscar nominations, *Cruel Intentions* managed

to win a few awards of its own, including the MTV Movie Award's Best Kiss category, awarded for Sarah Michelle Gellar and Selma Blair's famous French kiss, complete with lingering string of saliva connecting their lips.

Aside from being one of the only teen movies that openly referenced anal sex, oral sex and everything in between, *Cruel Intentions* will be remembered for its clever use of music. The soundtrack is awash with music from the era, featuring standout tracks from late-90s greats Fatboy Slim, Placebo, The Verve, Counting Crows and Blur.

Proving that what happens in the 90s should stay in the 90s, a TV reboot was filmed in 2016, with Sarah Michelle Gellar returning as nasty socialite and master manipulator Kathryn. The unaired pilot was never picked up, so fans of the film were spared the experience of revisiting a once-edgy premise that really does belong in another decade (along with Joshua Jackson's bleached-blond mane). Let's not even mention the two film sequels …

DAZED

and Confused

Alright, alright, alright! It may seem odd that a coming-of-age movie set in the 70s would become one of the biggest cult hits and cultural landmarks of the 90s, but when a film is good enough to end up on Quentin Tarantino's all-time favourite movies list, you know its cult status is unquestionable.

Released in 1993, Richard Linklater's *Dazed and Confused* follows the adventures of a bunch of Texan high schoolers navigating their final day of class in 1976. All the classic hallmarks of 70s teen behaviour are featured: drink driving, pot smoking, pinball playing, reckless climbing of towers and being ritualistically beaten by older, meaner jerks played by Ben Affleck.

The not-yet-star studded ensemble cast included Matthew McConaughey, Ben Affleck, Jason London, Parker Posey, Milla Jovovich, Adam Goldberg, Joey Lauren Adams and even Renée Zellweger in a blink-and-you-miss-it bit part.

Even though the film underperformed at the box office, its popularity slowly grew when released on VHS and LaserDisc in 1994. A clever, touching exploration of the teen scene in the 70s, *Dazed and Confused* has gone on to be played in college dorms and student lounge rooms over and over since its release.

Loaded with 70s anthems from Black Sabbath, Alice Cooper, Deep Purple and Lynyrd Skynyrd, the soundtrack went double platinum. Aside from introducing a new generation to the wonders of 70s rock, the film made all things 70s cool again, with stoner fashion standards such as tie-dyed tees and overalls making a comeback.

Possessing timeless appeal that spans generations, *Dazed and Confused* continues to age like a fine wine, much like Matthew McConaughey. Even after more than twenty years, this film and its cast still speaks to the teenager in all of us.

90s TRIVIA ALERT!

Vince Vaughn was considered to play the role of O'Bannion, one of the most hated characters in the history of 90s film. Ben Affleck was cast and did a brilliant job of playing the sad bully who is loathed by everyone, even his so-called friends.

31

WAYNE'S WORLD

Wayne's World! Party time! Excellent! On paper, *Wayne's World* shouldn't work. Full of bizarre dream sequences, improvised dialogue, outrageous plotlines and strange segues, the offbeat humour, incredible soundtrack, unique vernacular and endearing characters created a cult favourite and spawned a league of tragics who never, ever quoted their favourite movies. Not!

Debuting in 1992, *Wayne's World* stars Mike Myers and Dana Carvey as two lovable metalhead losers who host a low-budget public-access television show. The film also features Rob Lowe, Tia Carrere, Christopher Walken and the late Chris Farley, with rockers Alice Cooper and Meat Loaf also making memorable appearances.

A buddy movie about two young men who view the entire world through a pop-culture lens, references to big movies of the time (*Terminator 2*, *Jurassic Park, Field of Dreams*), classic television shows (*Bewitched, Laverne & Shirley*) and music (Queen, The Doors, Led Zeppelin, Aerosmith) backed up by other fixtures of 90s culture (crowd surfing, cable television) ensures that *Wayne's World* paints a vivid picture of youth culture in the decade before social media changed everything.

Just like *The Blues Brothers*, *Wayne's World* began as a *Saturday Night Live* sketch. Made for a modest US$20 million, the comedy ended up grossing more than US$121 million at the domestic box office. Despite a large number of celebrity cameos (including Steven Tyler from Aerosmith and 90s screen sirens Heather Locklear, Drew Barrymore and Kim Basinger), the 1993 sequel, *Wayne's World 2*, was less successful but still has its moments.

While some elements of *Wayne's World* might not translate perfectly into a contemporary context, both films are still genuinely laugh-out-loud funny and completely different from any other films made before or after they were released. After all these years, we're (still) not worthy!

REALITY BITES

Before he was Derek Zoolander, Ben Stiller directed a little indie film that ended up quietly defining the mood of a generation and teaching women all over the world to never bother dating men called Troy.

Starring 90s superbabes Winona Ryder, Ethan Hawke, Steve Zahn and Janeane Garofalo, *Reality Bites* encapsulates the experience of disillusioned twentysomethings living in America in a decade where selling out was a betrayal and slacking off was a noble pursuit.

Focusing on that tricky post-college period where everyone seemingly has it all figured out but you still have zero clue of what it means to be a successful adult, the film ticks off some very 90s plotlines including a HIV scare following a one night stand, the terror at coming out to your parents and incessantly calling the psychic hotline. Add in some baby doll dresses and oversized blazers, a cute pixie cut and lots of

cigarette smoking and ironic derision and you've got yourself a 90s fiesta.

Like many movies from the era, the soundtrack to this film was huge and ended up selling more than a million units. Remember, this was the era where you had to physically purchase cassette tapes or discs in order to listen to music. The soundtrack made The Knack's 1979 hit 'My Sharona' cool again for a hot minute and sent Lisa Loeb to number one with her love song 'Stay (I Missed You)'.

Despite most critics giving *Reality Bites* a lukewarm reception, the movie nonetheless has become a bit of a cult fave and an accurate reflection of what was on the mind of twenty-three year olds in the 90s. The memorable line 'Evian is naïve spelled backwards' points to how much Generation X mistrusted multinationals and struggled to take up meaningless jobs in the corporate world just to pay the bills. True to its title, reality really does in fact, bite.

SINGLES

Forget Matt Dillon and Bridget Fonda, the true star of this endearing early-90s romantic comedy is the city of Seattle. A love letter to the grunge scene crafted by director Cameron Crowe, *Singles* follows the lives of a group of cute twenty-somethings muddling their way through life and love (while frequently breaking the fourth wall to talk to the camera).

Featuring a landslide of flannelette shirts and long-haired rock gods, *Singles* is an all-out, unapologetic immersion in the world of 90s grunge. Going one notch higher than the movie in the popularity stakes, the *Singles* soundtrack is universally acknowledged as one of the greatest soundtracks of the decade. Released months before the movie hit cinemas, the soundtrack famously went platinum before the movie's cinematic release thanks to an 'all killer no filler' line-up of hits and B-sides from the likes of Smashing Pumpkins, Alice in Chains, Mother Love Bone, Screaming Trees and Paul Westerberg.

Apart from capturing the distinct energy, fashion and music of the 90s grunge scene, *Singles* offers a heart-warming glimpse into what dating was like in a pre-internet, smartphone-less world where people would sit at home desperately willing their landline to ring. While the heady world of 'video dating' (a thoroughly 90s phenomenon where single people would record introductory videos of themselves to be viewed by would-be suitors) provides many laughs, the universal experience of missed connections and love lost and found provides viewers of all generations with something familiar to hold onto.

90s CAMEO ALERT!

Look out for icons of the Seattle grunge movement Chris Cornell (Soundgarden), Layne Staley (Alice in Chains) and Eddie Vedder and Stone Gossard (Pearl Jam), who all make appearances in *Singles*.

TRAINSPOTTING

An edgy comedy focused on the lives of a ragtag bunch of heroin addicts living in a gritty part of Edinburgh might not seem like an obvious hit, but *Trainspotting* was just that and more to a generation of film fans.

A sensation on its release in 1996 (it was the second highest grossing British film of all time, after 1994's *Four Weddings and a Funeral*), *Trainspotting* followed the many, many, many trials and tribulations of Mark 'Rent Boy' Renton, Spud, Sick Boy, Begbie and other associated geezers. The fast-paced film was based on the 1993 novel by Irvine Welsh, directed by Danny Boyle and starred a relative newcomer Ewan McGregor. *Trainspotting* pulled the trick of tackling deadly serious issues like substance abuse, sexually transmitted diseases, parental neglect and infant death, while destroying viewers with a genuinely hilarious brand of black comedy.

Adored for its revered soundtrack of Britpop bangers, super sweary dialogue and several shocking scenes that really dialled up the gross-out factor (the scene involving a shit-encrusted toilet is truly gag-inducing), *Trainspotting*'s no-holds-barred attitude spoke to Gen-Xers who were looking to embrace anything anti-establishment.

Renton's famous 'Choose Life' opening monologue distils the mid-90s sentiment perfectly. Railing against the trappings of the consumerist world and safe, middle-class, suburban existences, Renton's speech gives the middle finger to meaningless careers, consumer goods, corporations, mortgages and routines.

A reminder that aiming to make millions, craft the perfect bod, grow a huge social media following and run ten companies by the time you're twenty-five are thoroughly modern pursuits, *Trainspotting* fully embraces the ethos of living in the moment, no matter what it costs.

PULP FICTION

Quentin Tarantino's ground-breaking cult hit debuted in 1994 and cemented its place within the pop-culture canon thanks to a unique screenplay, talented ensemble cast, very clever (and very sweary) dialogue and a sublime soundtrack packed with soul, funk and surf gems from the 60s and 70s.

While Tarantino was no stranger to Hollywood (by 1994 he'd already directed *Reservoir Dogs*, written *True Romance*, and played an Elvis impersonator in an episode of *The Golden Girls*), *Pulp Fiction* certainly signalled to Hollywood that he'd arrived.

A highly stylised film centring on the divergent lives of a couple of hitmen, a mob boss and his wife, and a prize fighter, *Pulp Fiction*'s narrative is punctuated with everything from acts of extreme violence, to darkly humorous, quotable conversations that have been memorised and recited time and time again by superfans ever since.

Considered to be a film that changed cinema forever, the phenomenal success and influence of *Pulp Fiction* inspired other independent filmmakers to chase commercial success (and many pretentious students to enrol in film school in the 90s).

Made on a modest budget estimated to be around the US$8 million mark, *Pulp Fiction* grossed more than US$213 million worldwide and remains one of IMDb's top-rated movies of all time. A comeback vehicle for veteran actors John Travolta and Bruce Willis, *Pulp Fiction* also starred Uma Thurman, Samuel L. Jackson and many of Tarantino's go-to actors, including Tim Roth and Harvey Keitel.

Winning a stack of major awards including the Cannes Film Festival's Palme d'Or, the Academy Award for Best Original Screenplay and the MTV Best Movie Award, *Pulp Fiction* was a runaway success embraced by mainstream audiences and critics despite featuring one of the most disturbing scenes to appear in a Hollywood film, ever. Struggling to remember what scene that could be? Do the words 'Bring out the gimp' ring any bells?

SHOWGIRLS

Dutch director Paul Verhoeven has built a career out of making shock-factor films slathered with liberal helpings of sex, violence and absurdist comedy. The 90s was a productive decade for Verhoeven, resulting in two mainstream hits, *Total Recall* and *Basic Instinct*, the criminally overlooked sci-fi action romp *Starship Troopers* and of course, *Showgirls* – a camp classic in the making.

An over-the-top affair from beginning to end, *Showgirls* focuses on the life of Las Vegas exotic dancer, Nomi Malone, played by *Saved by the Bell* star, Elizabeth Berkley. Co-starring Kyle MacLachlan and Gina Gershon, the film is largely celebrated for its cringe-worthy dialogue, gratuitous nudity and a particularly unforgettable sex scene in a pool that brings to mind a shark attack in *Jaws*.

Despite underperforming at the box office and receiving scathing reviews from critics, *Showgirls* had some tricks up its leather thong. It dominated the 16th Golden Raspberry Awards, 'winning' seven trophies including Worst Director. Verhoeven's surprise attendance at the event made him the first person to ever show up to receive a Razzie Award.

Showgirls also went on to become the highest grossing NC-17-rated film in the United States, reportedly earning more than US$100 million on home video (because home video was a thing in the 90s). Now categorised as an exemplary entry in the 'high camp guilty pleasure' genre, *Showgirls* remains a bedazzled, nipple-tasselled example of how 90s bad-taste films still have a place in the cinema canon today.

THAT'S SO 90S!

The erotic thriller

Thrillers featuring an obsessed, vengeful, unhinged (usually female) character really took off in the 90s. Following the solid foundation set up by the utterly terrifying *Fatal Attraction* in the 1980s, directors in the 90s took the erotic thriller baton and ran with it. Sure, the paint-by-numbers plots were often recycled, the acting hackneyed and the scores overly dramatic, but audiences lapped up the highly entertaining, very disturbing likes of *The Hand That Rocks the Cradle*, *Sleeping with the Enemy*, *Single White Female*, *Basic Instinct*, *Sliver*, *Poison Ivy* and *Fear*. Orgasms on rollercoasters, decapitation of family pets, gruesome deaths by stiletto and unauthorised breastfeeding of other women's babies are all calling cards that make this genre so damn memorable.

POINT BREAK

This epic surf-themed, bank heist thriller slash bromance from 1991 has earned its rightful place on many all-time-favourite films lists thanks to its big waves, exhilarating thrills, hot dudes, and some of the most quotable lines in movie history.

Starring the 90s dream duo of Patrick Swayze and Keanu Reeves and directed by future Oscar winner Kathryn Bigelow, *Point Break* wasn't exactly well received by critics – but thankfully audiences knew cinematic perfection when they saw it.

Following the undercover adventures of Keanu Reeves' buff FBI rookie Johnny Utah, who is hot on the trail of a brazen bank-robbing surf gang headed up by Patrick Swayze's spiritual ringleader and surf god Bodhi, *Point Break* sets a cracking pace from the start and never lets up.

Featuring great supporting turns by Lori Petty as the pixie-haired tough girl Tyler, Gary Busey as wise-guy veteran agent Pappas and a cameo from Red Hot Chili Peppers frontman Anthony Kiedis, *Point Break* is one of those cult movies with extreme rewatchability, even if you've already seen it fifty times or more.

Ignoring the fact that it's a universally terrible idea to try and rehash the classics, Hollywood's penchant for recycling movies resulted in a 2015 remake. Apart from being a Swayze-, Busey- and Keanu-free affair, the sloppy remake was a total wipe-out, ringing hollow with fans whose *Point Break* worship correctly remains limited to the original.

Show someone a rubber mask of an ex-president and chances are they'll reference *Point Break*. Visit Bells Beach, Australia, and someone will undoubtedly say, 'we'll get him when he comes back in' in an awful Australian accent. Decades later *Point Break* is still alive and kicking. May the sun never set on the greatest surf movie of all time.

TELEVISION

The decade where David Lynch scared the bejesus out of a generation, Darren Star and Aaron Spelling joined forces to hit multiple home runs, and the Vice President of the United States spoke out against the plotline of a major, prime-time series – the 90s was a huge era of television that left a lasting impression on the world. The decade in which powerful, intelligent women like Elaine Benes, Murphy Brown, Dana Scully and Buffy Summers proved that women could be key players in whatever career they chose (even vampire slaying), television in the 90s pushed boundaries, blew minds, opened eyes and converted a generation of viewers into life-long superfans.

SEINFELD

These pretzels are making me thirsty. The sea was angry that day my friend. Can you spare a square? No soup for you! Yada Yada Yada … No other series of the decade had the ability to work its way into our vernacular in the way that *Seinfeld* did.

The show about nothing burst onto the scene in July 1989 and then dominated the decade to come (it seemingly has never left our screens since). Centred on the lives of New Yorkers Jerry, George, Elaine and Kramer, *Seinfeld* successfully merged witty observations about everyday life with a dash of slapstick.

Covering everything from masturbation to double-dipping, the show was a genuine comedy phenomenon watched by millions. The show's success can partly be attributed to the comedy genius of co-creator Larry David, whose 'no hugging, no learning' mantra for the show ensured the characters started each episode afresh, never having evolved or learned their lesson.

Clever writing coupled with the enduring appeal of the four core characters ensured viewers kept coming back for more. People tuned in to see pathetic George Costanza hit all new lows and trouble-magnet and madcap hipster doofus Kramer create new calamities. To watch white-sneakered Jerry face his nemesis, Newman; and sassy Elaine deal with everything from dating egotistical men to handling impossible bosses.

Seinfeld's final episode may have aired in 1998, but the series is still a money-spinner for Jerry Seinfeld who reportedly earns in the vicinity of US$80 million each year in syndication fees alone. In the words of Cosmo Kramer, 'Giddy up!'

90s CAMEO ALERT!

Catherine Keener, Bette Midler, Teri Hatcher, Bryan Cranston, Debra Messing, James Spader, Sarah Silverman and Jeremy Piven all guest starred.

FRIENDS

Ross, Rachel, Monica, Chandler, Phoebe and Joey were a constant fixture in 90s homes. Everyone had a favourite character, everyone had an opinion on whether Ross cheated on Rachel when they were 'on a break' and many tried to emulate the sweet bachelor pad set-up – complete with twin recliners – that Joey and Chandler had going on for a while there.

Premiering in 1994, *Friends* was much more than a sitcom: it was a comforting warm blanket of familiarity viewers turned to for a decade. As the seasons unfolded, viewers got to know the characters' unique personalities and peccadillos as they caught up at Central Perk each week under the watchful eye of Gunther.

From Monica's need for control to Joey's cheesy pick-up lines, it's not a stretch to say that in the 90s, many viewers preferred spending time with the cast of *Friends* than with their own, real-life friends. As such, the show enjoyed huge ratings, with the episode titled, 'The One After the Superbowl' drawing an astounding fifty-two million viewers upon airing.

Apart from its significant impact on pop culture (people *still* say, 'How you doin'?', decades later), *Friends* made many people heinously rich: Warner Bros. reportedly still makes a billion dollars each year from syndication fees alone.

The catchy theme song performed by The Rembrandts had strong radio airplay leading to solid chart success. 'I'll Be There for You' may be a bog-standard pop-rock song, but never underestimate the selling power of being associated with a top-rating show and having the cast appear in your film clip.

In many ways, history hasn't been kind to *Friends*, with some contemporary audiences aghast at the fat shaming, sexism, homophobia and other borderline unacceptable themes and ideas presented by the show. But in other ways, the allure of *Friends* is stronger than ever. Constant re-runs; evergreen, relatable plotlines (love lost and found, room-mate dramas, career fails); and cute, on-trend again wardrobes have found *Friends* a whole new audience who missed it the first time around.

90s CAMEO ALERT!

Bruce Willis won an Emmy Award
for Outstanding Guest Actor in a
Comedy Series for his fleeting role
as Rachel's love interest.

THAT'S SO 90S!

Adult cartoons

Cartoons may have once just been for kids,
but in the 90s animated series for older
kids and adults took off. These shows were
comedies, usually with a darker, dirtier sense
of humour: *South Park, Rugrats, The Ren &
Stimpy Show, Beavis and Butt-Head,
The Simpsons* and *The Critic* were among
the biggest hits of the decade.

BUFFY
the Vampire Slayer

Not to be confused with the 1992 film starring Kristy Swanson and Luke Perry, Joss Whedon's *Buffy the Vampire Slayer* came to define the late-90s television zeitgeist dominated by a squad of strong, witty young heroines who slayed evil otherworldly forces while juggling schoolwork and boyfriends at the same time.

Because vampires and werewolves weren't always considered viable love interests (thanks *Twilight*), *Buffy the Vampire Slayer* centres on the experiences of a young woman with a talent for kicking vampire (and other demon) butt with the help of her friends, the Scooby Gang.

Buffy Summers (played by Sarah Michelle Gellar) hit our screens in 1997 and soon an army of diehard fans signed up to Team Buffy for a lifetime of adoration and worship. They hated bad guy Spike (until he came good, redeemed himself and hooked up with Buffy), watched with interest as the more introverted Willow found her feet (and superpowers), and were at a total loss years later when the series finale aired.

Apart from being a highly entertaining, well-written show filled with quotable dialogue, poignant moments and complex story arcs, this series was quietly responsible for many small-screen firsts. With TV depictions of lesbian couples still rare in the 90s, Willow and Tara's relationship set a pioneering example in a 'no big deal' kind of way. For a generation of viewers unaccustomed to seeing women in meaningful, loving relationships in their favourite shows, Willow and Tara's union represented a small, but not insignificant shift.

Starting a supernatural trend that lasted more than a decade, a year after Buffy became a household name, *Charmed* joined the fold by introducing us to a trio of witches who worked together as a force against evil from their San Francisco home. Buffy spin-off *Angel* would come later and rate even higher than its predecessor.

A favourite with academics, cosplayers, fan-fiction writers, Comic-Con attendees, pop-culture geeks and 90s tragics, all would agree that *Buffy* still slays.

THE X-FILES

Viewers first heard the distinctive opening theme to *The X-Files* in 1993, a haunting tune which would go on to permeate millions of lounge rooms for the better part of the decade.

Following the work of FBI Agents Fox Mulder (David Duchovny) and Dana Scully (Gillian Anderson) investigating paranormal cases involving UFOs, aliens, monsters, ghosts and the government's attempts to cover up all things extra-terrestrial, *The X-Files* dominated ratings, award shows and water cooler conversations for years.

Popular with conspiracy theorists, anti-government crackpots, Area 51 enthusiasts and believers in all things supernatural, the show's viewers quickly broadened outside the previously niche science-fiction audience. In the 90s, posters declaring 'The Truth Is Out There' hung on bedroom walls, 'I Want to Believe' T-shirts were worn and the term 'trust no one' became synonymous with the show.

Aside from the gripping mysteries and cryptic ideas presented on the show, the sexual tension between the two babes with FBI badges ensured viewers were always left wanting more.

X-Files episodes ran the gamut from interesting to absolutely terrifying: season two's 'The Host' (featuring a hideous, sewer-dwelling, half-man half–fluke worm mutant) left viewers afraid to use the toilet for weeks afterwards.

Looking back on the influence of *The X-Files*, one of the most interesting elements of the show was its skewering of gender stereotypes. Dana Scully is represented as an intelligent, capable, critical thinker who can not only handle a gun, but also resist the charms of Fox Mulder. In what has become known as 'The Scully Effect', *The X-Files* inspired a generation of girls to become scientists, cops, government agents and doctors, which is perhaps its greatest legacy of all.

90s TRIVIA ALERT!

Breaking Bad showrunner Vince Gilligan got his break writing an *X-Files* spec script. He was hired by creator Chris Carter and went on to pen some of the series' more memorable episodes. Gilligan eventually became an executive producer for the show and for *The X-Files* spin-off series, *The Lone Gunmen*.

FBI

TWIN PEAKS

Who would have thought that a surreal, mystery-slash-horror series featuring a bespectacled woman who channels messages through a log, a dwarf with a penchant for talking backwards and dancing, and a terrifying evil entity that turns people into murderers would end up becoming one of the decade's most influential television series?

As one of the most talked about shows of the 90s, *Twin Peaks* dominated water cooler and dinner party conversations thanks to its intriguing plotlines, coded dream sequences, eerie soundtrack and bizarre collection of memorable characters – some of which still haunt viewers' dreams.

Centred on out-of-towner Agent Dale Cooper's investigation into the mysterious murder of local high school homecoming queen Laura Palmer, the series took the whodunit crime procedural and gave it a supernatural, avant-garde makeover.

But what else would you expect when you've got a fearless writer and director like David Lynch at the wheel? With *Twin Peaks*, Lynch created a surreal yet familiar world that merged small-town diners and log cabins with big, creative (sometimes brutal) ideas that shouldn't work, but do when in the hands of a master like Lynch.

If you watched this show in the 90s then you almost certainly had a crush on hunky Bobby Briggs or sultry Audrey Horne, a fascination with The Log Lady, The Giant and The One-armed Man, and a morbid fear that BOB was lurking at the end of your bed.

Even though the 'Who killed Laura Palmer?' question has been answered, many people can't leave their obsession with this show behind, as evidenced by the annual celebration of all things *Twin Peaks* held in Washington each year and the huge interest the return of the series garnered in 2017.

Leaving a sizeable pop-cultural legacy, *Twin Peaks* will forever be associated with cherry pie, donuts and damn fine coffee; big glasses, plaid shirts and knitted sweaters; and the catchphrase, 'She's dead, wrapped in plastic', which was seemingly on everyone's lips in 1990.

NORTHERN EXPOSURE

Beyond the huge hits like *Friends*, *Seinfeld* and *Twin Peaks*, the 90s produced a lot of solid shows that may not have reached cult status with modern audiences but had a significant impact on viewers at the time. *Northern Exposure* is one of them.

Set in small-town Alaska, *Northern Exposure* was a light-hearted, Emmy Award winning CBS drama that ran from 1990 to 1995. Starring Rob Morrow, Janine Turner and John Corbett, the charming show centres on the life of Dr Joel Fleischman, a young Jewish doctor from New York City who ends up in Cicely, Alaska.

In a classic fish-out-of-water narrative prevalent in 90s television, Joel is a typical neurotic, east-coast hot-shot, unaccustomed to the realities of living in a small out-of-the-way town populated by eccentric, yet mostly lovable, residents. Of course, Joel grows to love the town and its people, as episode by episode he sheds his fears and big-city attitudes.

Along with the iconic moose wandering through town in the opening credits, the fashion and music, the overall 'Alaskan outpost aesthetic' of *Northern Exposure* is what many people remember most fondly.

Recently, many have been unknowingly channelling the *Northern Exposure* look as 90s fashion makes a comeback. Double denim, puffy jackets, vests, plaid shirts, Aztec print sweaters and trucker caps are the standard wardrobe of Cicely residents, and now also Brooklyn bartenders, Portland craft brewers and LA record-store owners.

Northern Exposure may not have broken the records that *Seinfeld* did, but it has a place in the heart of many viewers who came to see the residents of Cicely as a group of old friends you wish you never had to say goodbye to (especially the hunky community-radio DJ Chris Stevens, played by 90s heartthrob John Corbett).

MURPHY BROWN

This ground-breaking comedy may have first screened in 1988, but its defining moments definitely came in the 90s.

Starring Candice Bergen as a smart, outspoken TV network reporter, *Murphy Brown* deftly covered everything from single motherhood to cancer. But of course, no female-led show in the 90s could be bold enough to include a positive depiction of an intelligent, hardworking woman balancing a high-powered career with single motherhood without courting controversy.

Unsurprisingly, a male politician had a problem with the whole 'single motherhood' thing. American vice president Dan Quayle took aim at the show, saying it was 'Mocking the importance of fathers by bearing a child alone and calling it just another lifestyle choice.' Women collectively rolled their eyes at Quayle's out-of-touch opinion and he was rightly mocked for his retrograde view.

When Murphy's baby grew up, the character was played by Haley Joel Osment – before he went on to see dead people in *The Sixth Sense*. The show also featured a rotating list of celebrities running the desk as Murphy Brown's secretary, a quirky role filled by more than ninety different actors including Bette Midler, Sally Field and Michael Richards as *Seinfeld*'s Kramer in a clever crossover moment for the two hit shows.

Murphy Brown was a hugely popular, highly entertaining show beloved by critics and audiences alike. Case in point: Candice Bergen won so many Emmy Awards she removed herself from the running to give others a shot at winning.

Nostalgia has seen many shows from the 90s return and Murphy Brown is among them. The tan pantsuits and chunky turtleneck sweaters may be gone, but Murphy Brown still rules the airwaves.

90s TREND ALERT!

Murphy Brown wasn't the only smart sitcom to air that decade: *Herman's Head, NewsRadio* and *Frasier* were a trio of clever comedies that offered viewers something beyond the usual sitcom tropes and predictable jokes.

THE FRESH PRINCE
of Bel-Air

Now this is a story all about how a delightful sitcom stole the hearts of a generation and launched the career of a young actor into the stratosphere.

Running from 1990 to 1996, *The Fresh Prince of Bel-Air* signified an era of fun, light-hearted sitcoms never to be seen again. With the Fresh Prince, everyone had a good time – parents, grandparents, teens and tweens. It was the kind of show everyone could enjoy.

Following the life of Philadelphia teen Will Smith (played by … Will Smith), who is sent to live with his super-rich aunt and uncle, highfalutin' cousins Carlton and Hilary, and Geoffrey the butler, in an upscale mansion in Bel-Air. As a kid from the 'hood, much hilarity stems from watching Will learn the mysterious ways of rich people.

Responsible for some of the best on-screen fashion moments of the 90s, viewers were treated to a never-ending stream of colourful threads, bright caps and patterned prints worn by Will each episode. On the flipside of the fashion equation, cousin Carlton's preppy tennis whites and pastel knits – draped casually over his shoulders

– are a hilarious reminder of how different the cousins are.

Despite being at odds for most of the series, when street-smart Will and proper Carlton unite, magic happens. Performing in a Vegas dance competition under the names 'Will the Thrill' and 'Boogaloo Shrimp', the infamous sequence choreographed to Sugarhill Gang's 'Apache (Jump on It)' is one of the funniest moments of a six-year run. The scene remains a fan favourite and the moves are still regularly replicated on dance floors at weddings.

Despite not having much of a profile beforehand, Will Smith carries the series with ease, charisma and confidence. The show was so popular that, when it was cancelled after season four, the network had to reinstate it following a deluge of pleading fan mail.

The potential for a reboot has been raised, but with Will Smith being 50 years of age – and apparently unable to watch past episodes of the show without cringing – chatter surrounds the possibility of a Fresh Princess taking over the reins.

90s CAMEO ALERT!

The Fresh Prince of Bel-Air featured some big deal 90s celebrity guest stars, including Oprah Winfrey, Queen Latifah, Donald Trump, Boyz II Men, Chris Rock, Tyra Banks and Jay Leno.

SAVED BY THE BELL

The antics of the fresh-faced gang from California's fictional Bayside High School entertained many kids of the early 90s who were more than happy to overlook the stilted acting, cheesy lines and convoluted plots that characterised this wholesome comedy series.

Starring Mario Lopez, Tiffani Thiessen, Elizabeth Berkley, Mark-Paul Gosselaar and Dustin Diamond, *Saved by the Bell* follows the ups and downs of high school. Navigating exams, homework, sleepovers, summer jobs, parents and relationships, the core group of genetically blessed guys and girls graced our screens for a few short years before being spun off into several other less popular series and feature films including *Saved by the Bell: The College Years*, *Saved by the Bell: Hawaiian Style* and *Saved by the Bell: Wedding in Las Vegas*.

Watching this series outside of the era in which it was conceived is generally considered to be inadvisable, but die-hard viewers (and, of course, lovers of all things 90s) will enjoy marvelling at the incredible hairstyles, makeup and fashion sported by the cast. A parade of loud, patterned sweaters, double denim, jeans worn with high-top sneakers, vests, scrunchies and hairbands show just how earnestly awesome 90s looks were.

For such a happy-go-lucky, innocent show, *Saved by the Bell* is often dragged into the headlines due to some murky behaviour from cast members. Okay, cast *member*. While most of the gang have gone on to enjoy successful careers on stage and screen, Dustin Diamond (who played lovable nerd Screech) has served prison time for stabbing someone in a bar-room brawl and released a shockingly woeful sex tape entitled *Screeched: Saved by the Smell*, thus tarnishing many a beloved childhood memory of watching *Saved by the Bell* on Saturday mornings in the 90s.

BLOSSOM

Long before playing the neurobiologist partner of Sheldon Cooper on *The Big Bang Theory*, a baby-faced Mayim Bialik spent five years on our screens playing Blossom Russo, a young girl with a thing for sundresses, crochet vests and oversized, floppy bucket hats accessorised with, of course, a blossom.

A corny, heart-warming series that ran from 1990 to 1995 before being condemned to the sitcom graveyard, *Blossom* followed the journey of a sensible, smart girl being raised by a single father.

Admittedly, many teens watched *Blossom* primarily to swoon over dreamy Joey Lawrence, who reportedly received thousands of letters from fans each week (pre-Instagram fandom required a whole lot more effort).

Made before mobile phones, social media and the internet, much of *Blossom*'s appeal will be lost on current-day viewers. But at the time, *Blossom* did have incredible influence, especially on fashion. Suddenly, girls all over the world were dressing like Blossom in floppy hats, mixed prints and bold colours, and a *Blossom*-themed clothing line was released in department stores to cater to this market.

Complete with pink, cursive font, killer costumes and sweet 90s choreography, *Blossom*'s opening credits (performed by Dr John) provide a perfect snapshot of what family sitcoms from this decade were all about: sincerity, goodness, family values and having absolutely zero shame in performing elaborate, coordinated dance sequences with your friends and family.

ABSOLUTELY
Fabulous

First airing on the BBC in 1992, the outrageous exploits of Edina and Patsy emboldened a generation of women to forget about acting their age, embrace their flaws and have a truckload of fun while they can.

The complete opposite of what you'd call role models, Joanna Lumley's Patsy and Jennifer Saunders' Edina are comedic caricatures of London's fashion, media and PR set in the 90s.

Fond of alcohol, drugs, cigarettes, sex and calling each other, 'Sweetie, Darling', the duo pinball from personal crisis to personal crisis, as they obsess over ageing, dieting and maintaining their place within the In Crowd. All the while, Edina's long-suffering conservative daughter Saffron (played by Julia Sawalha) seethes away in the corner, scornfully judging her trainwreck mother and her friend.

Filled with over-the-top antics, off-the-wall scenarios and the butchering of some of the 90s wildest couture, *Ab Fab* relished its camp appeal, resulting in everyone from young gay men to senior citizens delighting in Patsy's and Edina's alcoholic, chain-smoking, recreational drug–abusing ways. International audiences agreed, with the show a hit with fans in Australia, the United States, Canada, France, Portugal and many other countries.

A long list of influential British celebrities from stage and screen clamoured to appear on the show, including Elton John, Stella McCartney, Naomi Campbell, Emma Bunton and co-creator Dawn French. If you look closely you'll even find a young Idris Elba in there.

No other series of the decade skewers the vices of the 90s quite like *Absolutely Fabulous*. This is the era before the pious #cleaneating trend took over, a time when you could flagrantly smoke indoors and when drinking during work hours was standard practice. Those heady days may be behind us, but we can always revisit them by watching *Ab Fab*.

THAT'S SO 90S!

Insane daytime TV

Reality-defying soap opera plots became almost the norm in the 90s. In *Days of Our Lives,* Marlena became possessed by the devil and proceeded to levitate and shoot thunderbolts out of her palms. Not to be outdone, *The Bold and the Beautiful*'s Taylor was kidnapped by the obsessed Moroccan Prince Omar and reassigned a new identity in the form of Princess Laila.

The other daytime staple, the talk show, really took a turn during the 90s, with the emergence of riotous shows filled with trash-talking, brawling folk. From paternity-test reveals to juicy revelations of cheating, and bizarre confessions of people having their lives ruined by their phobia of pickles, *Jerry Springer, Ricki Lake* and *Maury* collectively have much to answer for.

BEVERLY HILLS 90210

For teens in the 90s, the sweet sound of the *Beverly Hills 90210* intro (*da-na-na-na, da-na-na-na*, ch ch) was the international signal to get your butt on the couch immediately and stay glued there for the next hour.

Running from 1990 to 2000, the high-rating teen drama series created by television powerbrokers Aaron Spelling and Darren Star, focused on the lives of twins Brenda and Brandon Walsh who move to sunny California from the Midwest.

They meet a key group of classmates (who are meant to be teens, but some of those actors are *clearly* closer to thirty than they are to junior year) including smoking-hot bad boy with sideburns Dylan McKay (Luke Perry), all-American sweetheart Kelly Taylor (Jennie Garth), good girl Donna Martin (Tori Spelling), high-achieving Andrea Zuckerman (Gabrielle Carteris) and local chump with a tight, curly mullet, Steve Sanders (Ian Ziering).

They meet up at the Peach Pit for shakes, they discuss dramas by their lockers, fall in and out of love, protest to allow a student to graduate ('Donna Martin graduates!' is a rallying cry many 90s kids remember well) and suffer the deep shame of wearing the same black-and-white, off-the-shoulder dress complete with oversized novelty bow to the spring dance. Oh, the horror.

Beyond love triangles and spring dance–dress dramas, the series did a solid job of exploring more serious issues. Suicide, divorce, racism, date rape, teen pregnancy, drug abuse and parents exploding in car bombs were all covered in various plotlines with varying levels of success.

Syndicated everywhere from Spain to Serbia, the series was a worldwide hit but struggled to remain relevant when key cast members such as Shannen Doherty exited the show. Today, the series is a wonderfully nostalgic guide to 90s fashion, hair, lingo and music that will certainly be cherished and remembered by fans for decades to come (which is not something you can say about Darren Star's disappointing 2008 reboot/sequel *90210*).

MELROSE PLACE

Darren Star was on a major roll in the 90s, and his reputation for being a savvy creator of winning television dramas continued with *Melrose Place*. Airing from 1992 to 1999, *Melrose Place* was pure prime-time gold, pulling in solid ratings for most of its lifespan.

Starring Courtney Thorne-Smith, Josie Bissett, Marcia Cross, Grant Show, Andrew Shue and 'special guest star' Heather Locklear, *Melrose Place* was a more adult continuation of the *Beverly Hills 90210* universe that had a big impact on audiences who were soon hooked on the pure escapism offered by the heady world of 4616 Melrose Place.

Featuring a cute, Spanish-Colonial revival style apartment complex occupied by a selection of classic 90s studs and babes, the series crossover with *90210* was a brief one (Kelly from *90210* briefly appears in the beginning of *Melrose Place*, and hunky Jake appeared in a few, late episodes of *90210*) but it worked.

Critics weren't impressed with the frivolous, soapy plotlines but fans lapped up the

bitches, catfights and villains of *Melrose*. The genius promo tagline 'Mondays are a bitch' (adapted to 'Tuesday night's a bitch' in Australia) perfectly sums up the *Melrose Place* experience – audiences relished the overblown plotlines involving sociopathic baby-stealing women and double-crossing nasty bitches who will stop at nothing to 'get their man'.

Particularly memorable episodes include the apartment complex exploding into a ball of flames, trouble-maker Brooke (played by *Sex and the City*'s Kristin Davis) drowning in the apartment complex's pool, and the dramatic return of villainous rapist Richard who literally emerges from a shallow grave wearing a shiny new suit.

Television has well and truly moved on from this style of soapy prime-time series. One thing's for sure, there will never be another *Melrose Place* (even though they tried and failed to recreate it in 2009). While characters can successfully rise from the dead in *Melrose Place*, the series itself is best left in the 90s where it belongs.

MODELS INC.

Producer Aaron Spelling figured he was on to something good in the 90s, so he decided to wade into risky territory by creating a spin-off of a spin-off series. The equivalent of landing a quadruple Salchow jump in figure-skating, the chances of success were pretty slim but regardless, he gave it a shot with *Models Inc.*

Without the magic mojo of Darren Star, the trash-tastic series only lasted a year. An obvious attempt to cash in on the supermodel trend that swept the globe in the 90s, *Models Inc.* starred Linda Gray, Carrie-Anne Moss and Australian models/ actors Kylie Travis and Cameron Daddo.

Centred on the lives of the models, agents and photographers working in an LA modelling agency, *Models Inc.* was awash with pretty faces, fast cars, catwalk dramas, toxic relationships, smarmy millionaires and oh-so 90s couture.

More melodramatic soap than well-written drama, *Models Inc.* had all the hallmarks of bad TV: woeful acting, stilted dialogue, poorly written scripts and outlandish plotlines straight out of daytime TV.

Throwing everything but the kitchen sink at viewers, *Models Inc.* quickly descends into farce with blackmail, revenge killing, kidnapping, sexual assault, feuds, love triangles, sex slavery, murder and characters returning from the dead all being crammed into the confusing series.

It proved all too much for viewers who turned off in droves after being drawn in by the hype surrounding the series. Even though *Models Inc.* was cancelled a year after its launch, it remains an obscure look into the tail end of the *90210–Melrose Place* franchise and a cautionary tale of what happens when wealthy television producers fly too close to the sun.

THE NANNY

Premiering in 1993 and running until 1999, *The Nanny* struggled to find an audience in its first season but after finding its feet, proved to be a hit for CBS.

An original series created by Fran Drescher and her husband Peter Marc Jacobson, *The Nanny* drew heavily upon Drescher's experiences living in Queens, New York. A classic fish-out-of-water tale complete with canned laughter, the series covers the journey of Drescher's Fran Fine who is fired from her job at a bridal shop and ends up working as a nanny for the well-to-do Sheffield family.

With her big hair, loud voice and even louder outfits, the culture clash between a family of toffee-nosed Brits and a street-smart, Jewish–American woman is the basis for most of the show's comedy. The stereotypes are laid on thick and some of the long-running gags are laboured by the end of the series, but regardless *The Nanny* was a genuine hit with viewers.

While the pint-sized nanny from Flushing, Queens, was billed as the star of the show, the ensemble cast is what made this sitcom such a roaring success. Long-serving butler Niles, resident lovelorn desperado and troublemaker C.C. Babcock, and Fran's overbearing mother, Sylvia, all provided comic relief and contrast to the relatively tame Sheffield family of Maxwell, Brighton, Grace and Maggie. The spicy interactions between Niles and C.C. provided many of the show's most memorable zingers.

Arguably, the most interesting character of all could just be Grandma Yetta. Fran's chain-smoking grandmother lit up the screen with her over-the-top, flamboyant outfits and wicked banter. Almost always appearing with a cigarette in her mouth, tiny Grandma Yetta may have lost her first husband (Shlomo Rosenberg choked on a chicken bone) but in the series she finds love again with a dapper gentleman called Sammy, played by iconic recording artist Ray Charles.

Outlandish but endearing side plots such as this union between a forgetful Jewish grandmother and a blind music legend elevated *The Nanny* above the usual 90s sitcom fodder to a near-cult series.

90s CAMEO ALERT!

The Nanny might hold the record for number of celebrity cameos in a TV show, with Chevy Chase, Bette Midler, Elton John, Hugh Grant, Michael Bolton, Coolio, Joan Collins, Donald Trump, Whoopi Goldberg, Elizabeth Taylor and many more popping up in the series.

THAT'S SO 90S!

Unlikely celebrity hook-ups

**Forget celebrity power couples.
These brief and bizarre celebrity couplings had
everyone scratching their heads in the 90s.**

Madonna and Vanilla Ice

A decade in which Madonna thrilled fans with her *Blond Ambition* world tour, set up a record company, launched a much-talked-about book, made a documentary, released multiple albums that went platinum and starred in *Dick Tracy*, *A League of Their Own* and *Evita*, the 90s should have presented the Queen of Pop with many viable partners. Instead, in 1992 she dated Vanilla Ice (birth name: Robert Matthew Van Winkle) for nine, very weird months. The relationship may not have gone the distance but it was immortalised in Madonna's definitely not G-rated coffee table book, *Sex*, which Vanilla Ice later described as 'disgusting and cheap'.

Madonna and Dennis Rodman

By 1994, Madonna was dating professional basketballer and all-round wildcard Dennis Rodman. The union only lastet a few months, with Rodman going on to marry Carmen Electra in 1998 (before divorcing the following year) and bizarrely enough, forming a special relationship with North Korean leader Kim Jong-un.

THAT'S SO 90S!

Madonna and Tupac

In what may come as a surprise to some, rapper Tupac Shakur dated Madonna before he was killed in a drive-by shooting in 1996. Their relationship was mostly kept under wraps, that was until a hand-written break-up letter (a very 90s way to break up with someone) written by Tupac surfaced on the celebrity memorabilia auction scene in 2017.

Courtney Love and Ed Norton

Lead singer of Hole and former spouse of 90s grunge poster child Kurt Cobain Courtney Love and Academy Award–nominated actor Ed Norton may have seemed worlds apart but not only did they get together in the 90s, they also managed to stay together for a staggering four years (which is like forty in Hollywood years). After meeting on the set of *The People vs Larry Flynt,* the couple forged a relationship that perplexed many, but ultimately didn't go the distance. In the years that followed their break-up, Courtney Love's Twitter account has thrown love, hate and everything in between Ed Norton's way.

Lisa Marie Presley and Michael Jackson

A short-lived marriage truly from the WTF files, the union of the King of Pop and the only child of The King himself made the world collectively scratch their heads in amazement. Marrying in 1994, the marriage lasted only two years and will be best remembered for a cringe-worthy film clip featuring a naked Lisa Marie Presley and a supremely awkward kiss on stage at the MTV Video Music Awards.

Andre Agassi and Barbra Streisand

Before marrying fellow tennis champion Steffi Graf, Andre Agassi was linked to legendary singer, songwriter, actor and gay icon, Barbra Streisand. More than twenty-five years his senior, Streisand sent the tabloids into overdrive when she was spotted courtside at Wimbledon supporting her man. Although the relationship did not last, Agassi stated in his autobiography that, 'Dating Barbra Streisand is like wearing hot lava.' Whatever that means.

TECHNOLOGY

Once upon a time, we wandered the aisles of video stores, memorised phone numbers, spent hours on the landline talking to our friends, left awkward messages on answering machines, spoke to humans when ordering food and were forced to watch television episode-by-episode at a set time every week. It sounds utterly miserable, but with a Nokia in your pocket and a Discman in your backpack, anything was possible.

VIDEO STORES

Mention the words 'video store' to anyone who grew up in the 90s and their eyes will glaze over as they recall the simple pleasures that could be derived from a trip to Blockbuster on a Friday night.

Before Netflix gave us the ability to stream thousands of movies on demand in our own homes, at a low cost and with nearly zero effort, video stores were everything.

Wandering the garishly carpeted aisles of the local video store was a weekend ritual for many (so was 'accidentally' wandering into the porn section). Apart from having thousands of movies to choose from, there were also snacks to buy, free posters to nab for your bedroom wall and store attendants to develop awkward crushes on. Make no mistake about it, for a while there, for movie-lovers video stores were *the* place to be. Until they weren't.

As we all know, digital killed the video store. Of course, there's a sound reason for this. For a start, you had to leave your house. VHS tapes had to be rewound (be kind, rewind, folks!), DVDs sometimes skipped, and late fees were a killer. Waiting for one of a few copies of a new release to become available was pure agony. Anyone who frequented video stores in the 90s would be familiar with asking the shop assistant to check the returns box after seeing someone throw a few movies into the slot, hoping that they just returned that elusive copy of *Twister*.

Video stores also enabled dud movie experiences. Before websites like Rotten Tomatoes existed, selecting a movie was a perilous, anxiety-inducing process. Since you were stuck with your movie choice, a movie selection could make or break your weekend. In a decade where George Clooney was cast as Batman, rapper Vanilla Ice was given a feature film and such stinkers like *Stop! Or My Mom Will Shoot!* were made, hiring a movie was like playing Russian roulette.

Despite these shortcomings, video store nostalgia is still strong. While they are almost completely extinct, we're expecting some kind of resurrection any day now ...

90s TREND ALERT!

Anyone really hankering for the old Blockbuster experience will be pleased to know that there's a 90s video store–themed escape room experience operating in New Jersey.

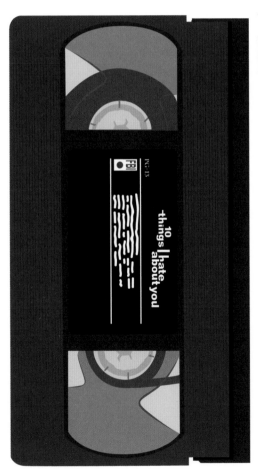

NOKIA PHONES

The beginning of the end of the landline telephone began in 1992, when Finnish consumer electronics company Nokia delivered a knockout punch to home phones around the world with the launch of the Nokia 1011.

Before phones were used for taking bathroom selfies, stalking exes on social media and cheating at trivia, they were used to make phonecalls (gasp!), send texts and spend an ungodly amount of time playing an embarrassingly simple but incredibly addictive game called Snake.

While the early Nokias had hard, sticky buttons; tiny, monochrome LCD screens; and a limited keypad that required the mastery of a bizarre multi-press typing style; this now Jurassic technology had some serious benefits in comparison to modern smartphones.

An epic battery life and lack of superfluous features meant users only had to charge their phone *once a week*. Renowned for their durability, Nokia 'brick' phones were practically indestructible in comparison to modern smartphones that seemingly combust into pieces under the slightest amount of pressure. While sneezing could cause modern smartphone screens to shatter into a million pieces, 90s Nokias could take a serious belting and even the odd dunk into a public toilet before being retired from service.

Despite being early innovators, Nokia haven't managed to keep up with smartphone giants Apple and Samsung. But those old ways are starting to seem attractive again. A generous battery life, indestructible nature and attractive price tag? Smartphone manufacturers take note.

CAR PHONES

Before mobile phones, talking on a phone while on-the-go was a pretty radical concept and there was nothing better to signify that you were a total hotshot than closing important business deals on your clunky car phone while driving your sports car.

Popular in the 1980s, car phones were still going strong in luxury vehicles in the early 90s, but sadly by the end of the decade the once cool-as-shit car phone was all but extinct.

Built into the armrest of vehicles made by luxury car manufacturers like Lexus, Renault and BMW, car phones were a signal of wealth and prestige. Associated with realtors, Wall Street traders, high-powered CEOs, trust-fund teens and celebrities, seeing a car phone was a big deal for the average person in the 90s – and using one was completely out of this world.

Of course, all good things must come to an end, and the emergence of the cell phone soon made car phones seem antiquated. With hot new flip phones by Motorola and high-tech Nokia 3210s out on the market in the late 90s, being seen talking into a heavy phone attached to a cord in your car was social poison.

90s TRIVIA ALERT!

Adding a nail to the car phone coffin, the Motorola StarTAC 1996 was the first flip cell phone to hit the market. With a discreet antenna, slimline body and lightweight clamshell design, the StarTAC was a must-have gadget in the mid-to-late 90s. Providing a dramatic way to end a phone call with a definitive *snap*, this was a phone that meant business.

DIAL-UP INTERNET

Aside from Nirvana and the Spice Girls, no other sound screeches 'the 90s' like the shrill static and whistling of a 56k modem dialling in to the network.

The early days of the internet were wondrous, innocent, hope-filled times; before trolls, online bullying, fake news, doxxing and those annoying 'sign up to our newsletter' pop-ups. In the 90s, dial-up internet was all there was and since there was nothing else to compare it to, surfing the World Wide Web at 28.8 kb/s seemed like magic.

Having to go through the process of connecting via a phone line may seem annoying but before the introduction of Wi-Fi and smartphones, accessing the internet (or 'logging on') was a novelty, a special event that might occur once or twice a week. And there were good reasons for this: dial-up internet speeds were painfully slow and the variety of pages on the internet was pretty limited.

Waiting for a page to appear on screen could take minutes, so anyone who ever used dial-up internet in the 90s would be familiar with walking away from the computer to make a cup of tea and returning to find the page still loading.

With the internet still in its infancy in the 90s, there was no Facebook, Reddit, YouTube, Spotify, TMZ, Netflix, Wikipedia, iTunes or any of the other countless ways we have today to lose hours online. News sites were very basic and early search engines like the now defunct AltaVista had limited capacity.

If you missed out on surfing the web in the early days, never fear. A few relics left over from the 90s can still be accessed, including the delightfully basic webpage for the 1998 rom-com *You've Got Mail* and CNN's incredibly dated main page for the OJ Simpson trial. Just don't try and use AltaVista to find them!

NINTENDO

All over the world in the 90s, parents struggled to get their children to clean their room, eat their dinner, complete their homework, study for that exam, call Grandma or listen to a goddamn word that they're saying … and Nintendo had a lot to do with that.

In the early 90s you were a very lucky kid if you had a Super Nintendo Entertainment System (SNES) or a Nintendo Game Boy. If you had both you were automatically crowned the king or queen of your neighbourhood. A sturdy, grey block of 8-bit awesomeness, Game Boys allowed users to take their gaming on the road, thus kickstarting many an addiction to *Tetris* (the *Candy Crush* of the 90s).

Hitting the market in 1996, the Nintendo 64 made home the most desirable place on Earth. Coming straight home from school was once the least preferable choice of things to do once classes finished for the day, but if there was a Nintendo 64 in your living room just begging to be played, you'd race home as soon as the school bell rang, throw your bag on the floor and fire up for a gaming session that lasted until your parents got home from work or your thumbs ceased to function, whichever came first.

Super Mario, *Mario Kart*, *NBA Hangtime* and *Mortal Kombat* were among the hottest games of the decade. Criminally underrated when it was released, *GoldenEye 007* (the companion game to 1997 Bond movie) has been hailed in more recent times as one of the greatest video games of all time.

In the 90s, unquestionably, the best cure for boredom was to fire up the Nintendo for a *Super Mario* session.

90s TRIVIA ALERT!

Before the Xbox vs PlayStation battle lines were
drawn, another console war split friendships. In
the 90s, you were either Team Nintendo or Team
SEGA. Although SEGA kids were never as cool as
Nintendo kids, the popularity of the 16-bit SEGA
Genesis (also known as the SEGA Mega Drive)
was boosted by the 1991 release of influential
game *Sonic the Hedgehog*. Years later in 2008,
Sonic struck a blow for SEGA by being voted the
UK's favourite computer game star of all time,
ahead of Mario, Donkey Kong, Pac-Man and
Pikachu. After all these years, the spiky-haired
blue speed demon is finally being paid his dues.

TAMAGOTCHIS

A 'digital pet', the Tamagotchi is a toy that requires its owner to be responsible, reliable and responsive to something other than themselves – so it's surprising that the labour-intensive game wound up becoming one of the biggest toy trends of the 90s.

Launched in 1996 in Japan (and 1997 in the rest of the world), Tamagotchi fever spread across the globe like wildfire. Tamagotchis were so damned popular some schools even banned them, as children were increasingly distracted with feeding and playing with their virtual alien spawn.

A digital companion that can be taken everywhere with you, the Tamagotchi became a substitute pet for kids who weren't allowed a real puppy of their own. Even kids with living, breathing pets started ignoring Fido in favour of their Tamagotchi … for a while.

Beginning with the exciting hatching of an egg, the Tamagotchi experience required users to care for their creature from birth to death by feeding, playing with, cleaning up after and giving medicine to their digital baby-slash-alien.

When the Tamagotchi's Hunger Meter starts lowering, simply feed it some bread. When the Happy Meter goes down, play a game with it. It was all so exciting in the beginning, seeing your baby alien grow and respond to feeding and play. But after the initial thrill, many kids grew neglectful, with the ominous skull icon appearing on screen to let you know that you've forgotten to feed your virtual baby for a few days.

Even though Japanese creator Aki Maita was rumoured to have kept a Tamagotchi alive for more than three decades, most were lucky to see out a year of life. But that didn't stop people from buying them. Just like the renewed hope and optimism that comes with starting a new relationship, people kept buying Tamagotchis in the hope that this time, they won't screw it all up.

90s REHASH ALERT!

Realising the mighty power of that
egg-shaped device, Japanese toy maker
Bandai re-released the Tamagotchi in 2017,
hoping that this time around a whole new
generation would sign up to have their time
and energy sucked up by a needy virtual
entity that rewards the user with …
well … nothing.

THE DISCMAN

Taking over where the cassette tape's Walkman left off, the Discman enabled a generation to continue ignoring their parents on long car rides by drowning out their voices with music.

Released by Sony in the 1980s, the Discman was a fixture of the 90s. Enjoying a decade of rule (before the MP3 came along and killed the compact disc) Discmans were a travel companion, a running buddy, a study helper and an absolute godsend on family road trips.

Anyone who owned a Discman understands the struggle of having to physically carry your CDs with you. The Discman was also limited by battery life, with the ominous blink of the 'low battery' sign dreaded by users desperate to listen to the Chili Peppers' 'Blood Sugar Sex Magik' for the fifteenth time in a row. And anyone who carried their Discman while jogging will remember the agony of a skipping disc (that is, before anti-skip technology was introduced).

But whatever the Discman lacked, it made up for in other ways. The Discman allowed users to fully immerse in an album. Limited by whatever CD collection they could afford, Discman users would punish an album over and over (and over) again, sometimes for years.

Indeed, the payoff of only having a handful of albums at your disposal is that you got to know those albums really, really well (even the secret track hidden eleven minutes after the album's supposed end).

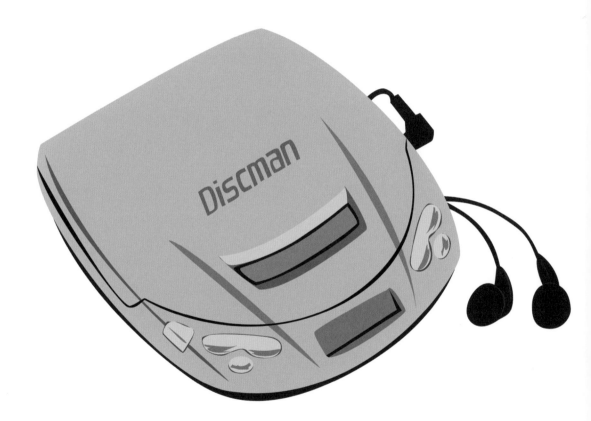

FOOD & FITNESS

A generation that glorified an apathetic approach to life ensured that health and fitness was never at the top of the mainstream agenda during the 90s, but a few key trends managed to cut through the indifference to shape the decade. From gliding along the streets in your rollerblades to sweating through a punishing Tae Bo session, then meeting your babe at Planet Hollywood for some sizzling fajitas followed by some fat-free yogurt for dessert, the 90s produced many crazes that didn't make it out of the decade alive.

WORKOUT VIDEOS

While not strictly a 90s phenomenon, workout videos reached all new highs (and lows) in the 1990s. Carrying over from their success in the 1980s, the 90s saw releases from the leg-warmer and lycra-clad likes of hyperactive Richard Simmons, stately Jane Fonda and perennially perky Denise Austin, in a series of workout videos that would help viewers to tone thighs, sculpt butts and fight flab all from the comfort of their living room.

Joining the stalwarts of the workout scene, supermodels Cindy Crawford and Claudia Schiffer capitalised on their fame (and largely unachievable body types) to release their own workout videos while Cher, Heather Locklear, Mark Wahlberg, Paula Abdul, Fabio, Jennie Garth and even La Toya Jackson also jumped on the bandwagon.

These videos serve as a horrifying time capsule of a decade where strapping on some leg weights and taking fitness advice from a singer or actor was an entirely acceptable practice.

90s CROSSOVER ALERT!

Even *Golden Girls* actress Estelle Getty released a workout video. Hitting stores in 1993, the *Young At Heart* VHS featured Estelle and a gang of seniors working out with the help of a young, hunky Frenchman. The video retailed for US$19.97 but the wisecracks and sexual innuendo came for free.

FAT-FREE FOODS

Pick any decade from the last 200 years and you'll find a weight loss trend that has since proven to be hokum. In the 90s, a war on fat was officially declared after some studies linked fat consumption to weight gain, cardiovascular disease and high cholesterol.

Packaged foods claiming to be '97% fat-free' started popping up in supermarkets, luring in dieters keen to drop a few pounds without starving themselves. Fat-free cheese, low-fat ice-cream, reduced-fat muffins and cookies – supermarket shelves were bursting with exciting new products that apparently allowed you to eat to your heart's content without gaining weight.

A 1993 episode of *Seinfeld* even catalogued this fat-free foods mania. Season Five's 'The Non-Fat Yogurt' episode depicts Jerry,

George and Elaine eating at a new yogurt store that sells delicious 'non-fat yogurt'. After putting on weight Elaine sends the yogurt to a lab for testing, only to discover that the yogurt contains fat after all.

Of course, we now know that many supposedly 'low-fat' foods are crammed full of other less-than-healthy ingredients such as sugar, salt and manufactured ingredients with long, unpronounceable names. We also now know that a wholesale ban on fat married with a carbohydrate, sugar and salt free-for-all is one way to fast track weight gain, not weight loss. Which is exactly what happened to people living in the Western world during the 90s. Despite the anti-fat hysteria, the world only got fatter.

ROLLERBLADING

From shirtless men gliding along beachfronts, to teens tearing around parks after school, for a moment there rollerblading, or inline skating, was hotter than hot.

Rollerblades hit the mass market in the 1980s, and by the 90s, old-school roller-skates with four chunky wheels and an unsightly front brake had been mostly superseded by the streamlined, thin-wheeled wonder of rollerblades.

Carrying on its tradition of exploiting trends to deliver marketable movies to the masses, Hollywood hopped on the blading bandwagon and released a few magnificently awful films in an attempt to capitalise on the popular pastime.

In 1990, teen heartthrob Corey Haim (may he rest in peace) starred in *Prayer of the Rollerboys*, an outlandish futuristic film that depicts a nasty, white supremacist gang of rollerbladers who deal drugs to minorities as a form of ethnic cleansing. Yep, that movie happened.

In 1993, Warner Bros. released another rollerblading genre film called *Airborne* (in which you can spot a very young Seth Green and a then-unknown Jack Black). The trend had officially peaked by 1998, but that didn't stop the Disney Channel from releasing *Brink!*, an earnest film about a boy who joins a competitive rollerblading team in order to save his family from financial ruin.

Unfortunately, rollerblading was never able to gain the street cred that skateboarding continues to enjoy (probably because of naff movies like *Airborne*). Just as rollerblading reached its peak in popularity, it became incredibly uncool, with many people abandoning their blades as quickly as they'd strapped them on.

Despite most people putting their blades into retirement, a select few refuse to allow those wheeled boots to gather dust. Every once in a while, like a mirage, a single rollerblader can still be seen on the horizon, blading their way into the sunset.

TAE BO

While the slacker vibe of the 90s certainly discouraged any form of physical exertion beyond moshing, skateboarding or wandering the aisles of the local video store, a few workout trends broke through the generational malaise to make an impact.

Combining martial arts manoeuvres and high-energy dance moves, Tae Bo was the brainchild of American actor, karate champion, one-time bodyguard and entrepreneurial fitness instructor, Billy Blanks. Devising the heart rate–raising, calorie burning workout in the late 80s, the Tae Bo business grew to epic proportions in the 90s thanks to celebrity endorsement (Paula Abdul was a big fan) and heavy promotion on infomercials.

Millions of Tae Bo branded videos flew off the shelves. Gyms started teaching Tae Bo workouts and followers flocked to the Billy Blanks World Training Center in Los Angeles to be whipped into shape by the master himself.

Before Cross-Fit, SoulCycle, HIIT and Wii Fit existed, slipping into a tank top for a sweaty Tae Bo session was the preferred way to blast your body into shape.

90s CAMEO ALERT!

Not content with just building a phenomenally successful fitness empire, Billy Blanks also starred alongside some of 90s Hollywood's biggest names. His movie appearances in the decade include The *Last Boy Scout* (alongside Bruce Willis), *Kiss the Girls* (with Morgan Freeman and Ashley Judd) and *Lionheart* (starring Jean-Claude Van-Damme).

THE SODA WARS

Proving that short-lived fads and one-hit wonders aren't limited to the fashion and recording industries, the 90s saw soda manufacturers launching a series of 'new and improved' drinks in an effort to dominate the carbonated drink market. Most were abject failures.

Several brands made a tilt at creating transparent, colourless beverages in the 90s with both Tab Clear and Crystal Pepsi emerging in 1992. Despite huge marketing campaigns including Superbowl ads, Crystal Pepsi was doomed to fail thanks to Coca-Cola's infamous kamikaze marketing of Tab Clear. Deliberately creating and launching a product so awful that it dragged the entire clear-soda market down with it was the type of next-level evil-genius marketing ploy that would make late, great comedian Bill Hicks weep.

Launched by Coca-Cola in 1993 and discontinued only two years later, OK Soda was an obvious attempt to capture the notoriously cynical Generation X market using non-traditional marketing tactics.

Predictably, a generation known for their deep mistrust of multinational corporations saw right through the cash grab and Coca-Cola soon admitted defeat after poor sales in test markets.

Not having learned their lesson, 1994 saw Coca-Cola launch Fruitopia in yet another attempt to capture the youth market. Flavour names like Tangerine Wavelength, Citrus Consciousness, Fruit Integration and Banana Vanilla Inclination were a nod to 60s hippie culture that was lost on many and the brand fell out of favour by the 00s.

In 1997, a new-age beverage called Orbitz hit the shelves with the perplexing tagline 'The drink with balls'. A fruity potion filled with floating, gelatinous balls, Orbitz came in strange flavour combinations including Pineapple–Banana–Cherry–Coconut. Consumers decided they'd prefer not to have weird, slimy balls in their drinks and Orbitz was a flop. Decades later, bubble tea is a serious trend – so maybe Orbitz was simply a visionary product released before its time?

BOTTLED WATER

One of the most alarming examples of marketing's incredible power has to be the multi-billion-dollar bottled water industry. Selling consumers a packaged version of something that can be accessed for free in most parts of the Western world, is both pure marketing genius and environmental vandalism.

Bottled water was marketed to the masses long before the 90s, with brands such as Evian and Perrier enjoying popularity in the 70s and 80s, but in the 90s, the industry took things to the next level with clever marketing, questionable health claims and celebrity endorsement.

Realising that soda sales were tapering off due to more health-conscious consumers, the big soda manufacturers such as Coca-Cola and PepsiCo made a successful play for the bottled water market, and made billions in the process.

As the trajectory of bottled water sales continued its meteoric rise, plastic bottles began clogging waterways and washing up on beaches. The Great Pacific Garbage Patch located between Hawaii and California started to grow at a faster rate than ever before. Despite this, our collective thirst for buying bottled water from vending machines and supermarkets only grew.

While the market won, the environment did not, and the world is now paying the price. If there's one trend that definitely should have been left behind in the 90s, it's bottled water.

CAPPUCCINOS

Long before unicorn lattes, matcha tea, hemp milk smoothies and bulletproof coffee were in, a humble caffeinated beverage from Italy became the drink order of the decade thanks to two food trends colliding at the same time.

In the 90s, Italian cuisine experienced a resurgence in popularity across America and the world. Pasta, pesto, sundried tomatoes and garlic bread were all on high rotation on restaurant menus. Concurrently, coffee houses, espresso bars and cafes were booming, with people flocking to their local coffee joint to hang out, go on blind dates and attend poetry slams.

As such, coffee shops were a fixture of 90s movies and television. The gang from *Friends* met up at Central Perk and the cast of *Frasier* spent plenty of time at Café Nervosa, their local, upscale coffee bar. Perhaps the best representation of 90s coffee culture features in Steve Martin's 1991 comedy *LA Story*, lampooning obnoxious coffee orders including a 'double decaf cappuccino', followed by a 'half double decaffeinated half-caf, with a twist of lemon'.

The public's newfound love for the super-foamy, chocolate-dusted beverage wasn't limited to coffee shops. A new wave of home espresso machines popped up across the world, giving 90s dinner party hosts a new way to impress their guests. Cappuccino sachets containing an ungodly mixture of instant coffee and powdered milk also became common in workplaces that didn't have a coffee-vending machine magically dispensing searing hot, watery cappuccinos at the touch of a button.

A trend that flamed out once the third wave of coffee culture arrived with its emphasis on artisanal cups not doused in chocolate dust, cappuccinos are still found on menus throughout the world, but these days tend to be the type of coffee your small town–dwelling aunt orders at the Olive Garden when she's visiting the big city.

FOCACCIA

The 90s was a blissful decade where carbs were not the enemy and gluten wasn't yet demonised. It was a glorious time to be alive, where one could freely order a sandwich or grab a slice of pizza without feeling the shame associated with carb consumption that has led to such monstrosities as bun-less burgers.

The Washington Post called it in a January 1994 with the headline 'It's flat. It's Italian. It's not pizza. It's focaccia – coming to a bread basket near you'. While all types of baked goods were on the menu in the 90s (pop tarts, burger buns, hot pockets, crusty baguettes), focaccia was undoubtedly the bread of the decade.

With roots in ancient Rome, focaccia took off due to a resurgence in artisanal baking and the renewed interest in Italian fare. In previous decades, diners were happy with run-of-the-mill, somewhat flavourless, sliced white bread bought cheaply at supermarkets, but 90s diners wanted something more.

Viewed as a sophisticated choice at the time, the versatile herbed bread (which, let's face it, is a far-cry from the real Italian stuff) found its way to café menus, speciality food stores, dinner party spreads and restaurant bread baskets around the world. Thick slices of focaccia were filled with semi-sundried tomatoes, marinated olives, pickled artichokes and salami and squashed into many a sandwich press in America and beyond.

Focaccia fell out of favour in the 00s when the low-carb trend rendered bread-eating a diet sin. The king of breads in the 90s, focaccia has never really recovered from its dethroning, yet still remains a fixture in Italy where the real stuff has been appreciated for thousands of years.

PLANET HOLLYWOOD

Celebrities selling their souls to flog goods and services they don't believe in is nothing new, but during the 90s this trend manifested in a hot run of themed restaurants part-owned by celebrities.

Launched in New York in 1991, Planet Hollywood was the biggest player in the celebrity-endorsed eatery gambit. Dreamed up by Hollywood movie producer Keith Barish (who produced *The Fugitive* and *Sophie's Choice*), the restaurant chain was a joint venture between Barish, Hard Rock Café owner Robert Earl and celebrity stakeholders Sylvester Stallone, Bruce Willis, Arnold Schwarzenegger and Demi Moore.

From Sydney to London, Cancun and beyond, more than 90 Planet Hollywoods popped up all over the world. Featuring garish dining rooms packed with movie memorabilia, stepping into a Planet Hollywood outlet in the 90s was an assault on the senses. And then came the menu.

Featuring bland, inoffensive American standards such as nachos, cheeseburgers and 90s classics like huge bowls of creamy pasta and chicken fajitas that arrived on a sizzling hot plate, the food at Planet Hollywood was run-of-the-mill chain restaurant fare window-dressed with star-studded celebrity openings attended by 90s celebs like Charlie Sheen, Christian Slater and Wesley Snipes.

Despite this, crowds of people flocked to Planet Hollywood … for a while. Proving to be more of a novelty and less of a sustainable business model, the chain dwindled towards the end of the decade after a series of setbacks including two bankruptcies. Today, only six, stripped-back Planet Hollywood–branded businesses remain, including the Planet Hollywood Resort and Casino in Las Vegas. It appears that, just like an ageing has-been entertainer, Planet Hollywood is living out its days under the neon lights of Vegas.

THAT'S SO 90S!

Celebrity owned restaurant chains

The 90s celebrity eatery action wasn't limited to Planet Hollywood. Country music star Kenny Rogers opened chicken fast-food chain Kenny Rogers Roasters. In the same decade, the short-lived, sports-themed Official All Star Cafe opened with the backing of Wayne Gretzky, Andre Agassi, Shaquille O'Neal and Monica Seles. While eating and modelling aren't exactly compatible, supermodels made a play for the food dollar with the Fashion Café. Launched at New York's Rockefeller Center in 1995, Fashion Café was owned by Italian siblings Francesco and Tommaso Buti and fronted by Naomi Campbell, Elle Macpherson, Christy Turlington and Claudia Schiffer, only to end on a sour note a few years later when the Buti brothers were indicted on fraud charges. Undoubtedly, the heavyweight title for the strangest celebrity eatery of the decade belongs to Hulk Hogan's Pastamania. Opened at Minnesota's Mall of America in 1995, despite serving Hulk-shaped pasta called 'Hulkaroni', Pastamania flopped, closing only months later.

COCKTAILS

In the 90s, going to bars to *gasp* meet someone and talk face-to-face was still a genuine way to find yourself a potential romantic partner. The preferred way to boost your confidence and blow off steam after work, the decade saw cocktail drinking reach all new heights.

When it comes to spirits, vodka was undoubtedly the spirit of the 90s. While the martini was nothing new, many bastardised forms of vodka martinis started popping up. Appletinis, crantinis, espresso martinis, raspberry martinis, watermelon martinis and French martinis were on bar menus everywhere.

A close relative of the crantini, the Cosmopolitan really took off late in the decade, thanks to the popularity of *Sex and the City*. First appearing in the series in 1999, the sweet, pink Cosmo soon became the drink most associated with the New York foursome's outings to Manhattan's hottest bars and clubs.

While sugar wasn't exactly considered a health food in the 90s, it wasn't yet the major enemy that it has since become. So drinkers were happy to emulate Carrie and the gang by ordering sweet-yet-tart Cosmos to their hearts' content.

By the mid-00s, along with *Sex and the City*, the Cosmopolitan was on its way out. Outside of the 90s (and Las Vegas), most drinkers wouldn't be caught dead with a bright pink cocktail in their hand.

A drink that defined a decade, the Cosmopolitan can still be found lingering on dusty bar-room cocktail lists, where occasionally, one shameless patron orders one for old time's sake.

FASHION

Flannel shirts and ripped jeans, Timberland boots and baggy pants, tartan miniskirts and long socks, a black velvet choker and Doc Martens boots; the 90s produced many fashion combos that still have a place in many wardrobes around the world. And there are the looks we'd all like to forget…

FLANNEL SHIRTS

Once worn by everyone from lumberjacks to construction workers and outdoors-loving grandpas, the flannel shirt was adopted by the grunge and alternative music scene in the early 90s and soon became the calling card of the grunge era.

Once the counter-cultural music movement spread beyond Seattle out into the wider world, young adults all over the globe began dressing like musicians from the Pacific Northwest, namely the late Kurt Cobain. Acquired from thrift stores, yard sales and parents' wardrobes, flannel shirts were a cheap, long-lasting fashion all-rounder that suited the practical nature of most grunge wardrobe choices.

Worn buttoned up, over a band tee, or tied around your waist when it got too hot, the unisex flannel shirt was the standard uniform of the decade. Typically paired with the ubiquitous combo of ripped jeans and Converse sneakers or Doc Martens boots, you could wear a flannel shirt to a music festival, the movies, school, college, and a family dinner at the local pizza shop – it was a comfortable, trusty go-to that never let you down.

Fashion pundits reviewing the style choices of the grunge era through a contemporary lens often give way too much credit to the thought processes that went into the outfits of the decade. Mostly, not a lot of thought went into what was being worn.

Nowadays, many wardrobes are carefully curated by people who put hours into crafting a look that gives off the 'just got out of bed' vibe, but in the 90s most people into grunge really did just roll out of bed and grab a well-worn flannel off the floor. And forget about updating your wardrobe each season because wearing the same faded, ripped shirt until it disintegrated was par for the course in the 90s.

Flannel shirts are still on high rotation in contemporary wardrobes, but they're more likely to cost a hell of a lot more and be paraded on the back of a Silicon Valley start-up dude bro trying to appear 'authentic' than a permanently stoned bass guitarist whose stringy long hair hasn't been washed in weeks.

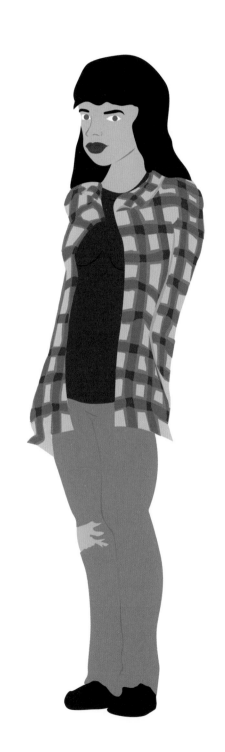

CHOKERS

If you were a young woman in the 90s, at some stage you probably wore a choker. Which means that at some stage your parents (or other narc adult figure) asked why on earth you're wearing that dog collar around your neck?

A fashion accessory that seems to rise from the dead every decade or so, chokers have adorned the necks of women for aeons. Once considered a symbol of death by guillotine (eeeek!) the choker has managed to shake off its bloody connotations to be embraced by the mainstream fashion world. From the parlours of eighteenth-century Britain to the red carpet events of Hollywood in the 90s, the appeal of the choker crosses continents and centuries.

In the 90s the choker took on a post-punk, grunge twist. Whether it was a cheap piece of thin black velvet acquired from a fabric store or a thick, jewel-encrusted number for special occasions, chokers were worn in classrooms, on prom nights, to music festivals, probably even job interviews. Such was life in the 90s.

Even though Instagram and reality TV shows hadn't been invented yet, celebrity influence was still incredibly powerful. Drew Barrymore, Naomi Campbell, Winona Ryder, Shannen Doherty and Reese Witherspoon were all choker wearers and even Kate Winslet wore one to the 1998 Golden Globes. With all the 90s It Girls wearing chokers on magazine covers, to movie premieres and while on set, teens everywhere from suburban Australia to rural Idaho followed suit.

The choker took a break in the 00s when it went into hibernation, lying dormant while waiting for its next stint in the spotlight. It didn't need to wait long. By 2014 the choker was back on the necks of women worldwide thanks to the likes of Beyoncé and Taylor Swift indulging in a little 90s nostalgia.

DOC MARTENS BOOTS

A footwear brand with serious staying power, Doc Martens may not have been a new thing in the 90s, but they were definitely a cool thing.

First hitting shelves in the 60s, the heavy, lace-up leather boot was originally worn by working-class factory workers but soon began to gain street cred elsewhere. Associated with the skinheads of the British punk scene in the 70s, Doc Martens have gone on to enjoy a long relationship with music movements ever since.

Despite the boot's popularity waxing and waning over the years, come the 90s, Doc Martens were back with the In Crowd yet again. Worn with everything from baby doll dresses to ripped jeans, Doc Martens were the boot of choice for grunge-scene regulars of all genders.

So why did the humble boot surge in popularity during the 90s? Unlike many other fashion trends, Docs are incredibly practical shoes. A pair of sturdy, steel-toed Docs are the ideal companion of any festival-goer. Not only do these trusty boots protect your toes from being stomped on in the mosh pit, they also hide your feet from common gig-related liquids such as beer and vomit (while looking infinitely better than a pair of sensible Hush Puppies).

With punk-rock credentials and a track record of keeping the feet of rock fans safe from harm, it makes sense that Doc Martens were so popular during the grunge era, a time when music taste informed so many fashion choices and a good pair of nearly indestructible boots would see you through even the muddiest of Lollapaloozas.

'THE RACHEL'

Ask any hairdresser who worked through the 90s what the most requested haircut of the decade was and you'll hear a long groan followed by the weary words: 'The Rachel'.

In 1994 *Friends* star Jennifer Aniston appeared on screen sporting a long, layered shag bob, and little did she know that her new haircut was going to be replicated by women all over the world for years to come. As one of the most hyped shows of the decade, *Friends* had a strong influence over fans who enthusiastically emulated the fashion and lingo of their favourite show.

Despite Aniston only sporting the signature hairstyle for the first few seasons of *Friends*, the cut took on a life of its own and replicated like a virus. To make things worse, the haircut was only well suited to certain face shapes and was especially difficult to style. Everyone from teenage girls to high school teachers got burned by the high-maintenance cut that was notoriously awkward to grow out.

As future seasons of *Friends* unfolded, Rachel Green wore her hair long and poker straight, then in a short, sharp bob – but regardless of how many different hairstyles she wore, 'The Rachel' is the one the public latched onto and refused to let go of, much to Aniston's dismay.

90s TRIVIA ALERT!

Confounded by its popularity, Jennifer Aniston famously told *Allure* magazine in 2011 that it was not only not her best look but, 'How do I say this? I think it was the ugliest haircut I've ever seen.'

THE CAESAR CUT

Named after Roman politician Julius Caesar who rocked this haircut in ancient times – before being assassinated in 44BC – the Caesar cut had a red-hot run with discerning men in the 1990s when the style's popularity reached its zenith.

An era-defining haircut characterised by short, horizontally-cut bangs pushed forward over the forehead (perfect for concealing receding hairlines), the Caesar cut presented a low-maintenance style that worked well with different face shapes and hair types. The cut is easily spiced up with variations: the Messy Caesar achieves that tousled, just-got-out-of-bed look (that actually took a while to create); while the Mod Caesar is a bit rock 'n' roll (think Noel Gallagher).

Sported by the likes of George Clooney, Justin Timberlake, Antonio Banderas, Billy Zane and Eminem, hairdressers would have crafted countless Caesar cuts in the 90s. Yet just like the figure it was named after, the haircut enjoyed a brief reign in the 1990s before being knocked off its perch by other contenders, such as the buzz cut.

Of course, the difference between Caesar the man and Caesar the haircut is that the hairstyle has had the opportunity to live on again in another decade, on another head. Namely the head of Canadian rapper Drake, who somehow makes the modern-day Caesar cut look better than ever before (sorry Julius).

PLUCKED EYEBROWS

If there's one thing that many women regret doing in the 90s (apart from dating a guy called Chad/Brad/insert entitled douchebag's name here), it's declaring war on their eyebrows.

The big, bushy brows of the 80s fell out of favour, to be replaced in the 90s by the pencil-thin look embraced by everyone from Gwen Stefani and Drew Barrymore, to Kate Moss and Sarah Michelle Gellar.

Now considered a bit of a beauty sin, some people in the 90s accidentally ended up with thin eyebrows due to overzealous plucking – one hair here, then another one there, then another to even out the look, and – oooops! – where did my brows go? Others purposely waged full-scale devastation on their brows by waxing and tweezing, then pencilling in a line to replicate a thin brow.

No matter whether you arrived there by accident or intention, the end result was always the same: permanent, irreversible brow damage. By the 00s, thin brows were on the way out, but the damage was already well and truly done.

As with most fashion and beauty trends, what is old becomes new, and big 80s brows started booming once again. Eyebrow makeup, brow builders and even eyebrow transplants were enlisted to remedy the fallout of the great eyebrow purge of the 90s.

They say that those who don't learn from history are doomed to repeat it, so if you take one thing away from the decade it's this: step away from the tweezers and leave your goddamn eyebrows alone.

TIMBERLAND BOOTS

Perfect for working on construction sites and trudging through snow, the humble, waterproof Timberland boot experienced a huge surge in popularity in the 90s. Sales saw a threefold increase in the decade that Timberlands expanded beyond their 'great outdoors' market to become a street-style must-have.

But why did a practical boot invented decades before suddenly emerge as one of the shoes of the decade? Well, Timberland Company partly has rap and hip-hop artists to thank for kickstarting its renaissance.

Biggie Smalls rapped about them. Wu-Tang Clan wore them on stage and Tupac donned them on the red carpet of the 1993 Soul Train Music Awards. Sales of Timberland boots took off and soon enough, wearing a pair of wheat-coloured Timberlands with oversized baggy jeans and a durag (or in Tupac's case, double denim and a 'thug life' beanie) was all the rage.

Once only found on the feet of blue-collar builders and carpenters, the 90s signalled the Timberland boot's successful migration to the high street where they have happily lived ever since. Because who wouldn't love a great-looking, long-lasting, hard-wearing, waterproof boot that keeps your feet warm and dry and can be cleaned with an eraser? Biggie and Tupac were definitely onto something.

90s CROSSOVER ALERT!

The Timberland Classic 6-inch boots were so popular in the 90s, Nike, Reebok and even Adidas dipped their toes into the outerwear-hiking boot market in an attempt to compete. Clearly none of them succeeded.

HYPERCOLOR

T-shirts

A fashion experiment that afflicted many school kids regardless of gender, the Hypercolor T-shirt craze swept the world by storm, then faded out as quickly as their signature heat marks.

Produced by Seattle-based Generra Sportswear Company, the range of heat-sensitive T-shirts (and shorts, pants and tights) hit stores in 1991 and promptly sold millions thanks to kids pestering their parents to buy them the latest, must-have T-shirt.

The concept was simple: marketed as a 'metamorphic color system', when touched with a warm hand the T-shirt would react and change hue ... cool, huh? Well sure, a perfectly placed handprint mark on a tee looks kind of cool, but the shirt produced a few problems that only became evident once you had it on your back.

Women and girls with big boobs soon realised that Hypercolor was a cruel wardrobe choice, as walking around with two obvious, brightly-coloured marks on your chest resulted in excruciating social death. Also, during summer Hypercolor T-shirts only emphasised your sweat patches – not something anyone really wants to draw attention to.

Another problem with the fabric arose upon washing. Run a Hypercolor tee through a hot cycle and the magical, Hypercolor properties would be ruined forever – leaving the owner with a malfunctioning, faded shirt that can't perform any of the magic tricks it's supposed to.

The Hypercolor brand dissolved almost as quickly as it appeared, with the company going bankrupt only a year after shifting millions of units. Generra made the error of trying to expand the range aggressively just as the brand was losing its street cred and consumers were turning away in droves. Remnants of millions of Hypercolor tees now rest in peace in landfill sites around the world.

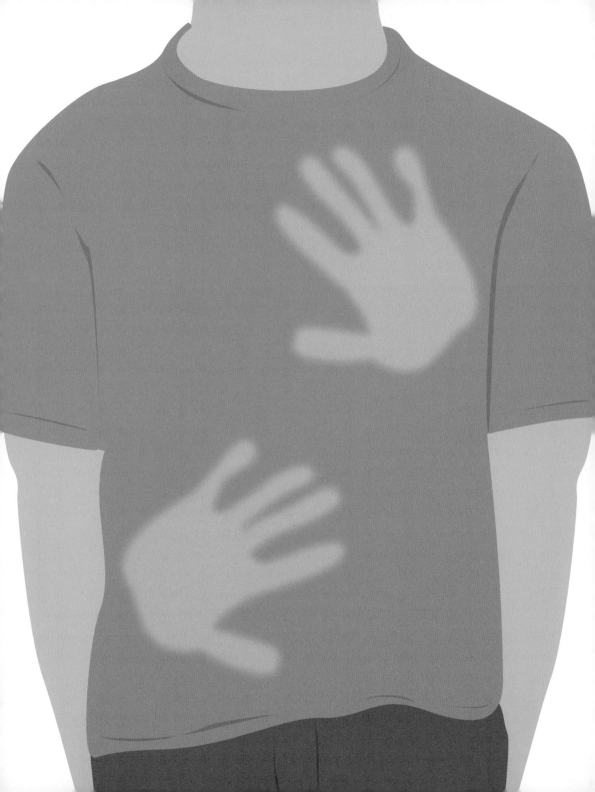

FROSTED TIPS

Regarded by many as one of the more heinous fashion crimes of the decade, this late-90s men's hair trend can pretty much be blamed on boy bands. While taking over the world's radio stations and creating mass hysteria at shopping mall appearances, many of these crushable boys did so sporting a ubiquitous short, spiked cut with peroxide-blond ends.

Definitely one from the 'what were they thinking?' files, many a male music star fell for frosted tips, with Justin Timberlake and Lance Bass from NSYNC, AJ McLean from Backstreet Boys, Mark McGrath from Sugar Ray and child prodigy Aaron Carter all embracing the look.

Mercifully, the trend was relatively short-lived, petering out by the early 00s when men began to step away from the bleach in favour of a more natural look.

Just like a horror-movie bogeyman who can never be killed, frosted tips have tried to wage a comeback to claim more innocent victims. As recently as 2017, frosted tips were listed as a 90s hair trend on the comeback trail. Despite contemporary fashion websites trying to make frosted tips a thing again, the peroxide pineapple look thankfully has never managed to gain the same foothold it did in the 90s.

You've been warned. Frost your tips once, and it's an innocent mistake. Frost your tips the second time around and you deserve whatever comes your way (probably green-tinged hair if you frequent chlorinated swimming pools).

BABY-G WATCHES

While the Swatch watch indisputably ruled the wrist in the 80s, in the 90s it was dethroned by the Baby-G.

Launched by Casio in 1994 as a companion to their super popular, more masculine G-Shock, the Baby-G was marketed to young women as a lightweight, hard-wearing watch that was also shock- and water-resistant.

Available in a kaleidoscope of colours including pastel pink, pale purple, bright orange and canary yellow, by the mid-90s Baby-G watches were on the wrists of millions of middle-school kids and teen girls all over the world. Anyone who didn't have one, was likely begging their parents for one – such was the pester power of the Baby-G.

More than just a watch, Baby-Gs were a fashion statement, a must-have accessory that showed the world you were one of the cool kids. Thankfully, for many young women, the chunky, plastic timepiece was within striking range thanks to a reasonable price point that ensured it was a genuine gift possibility come Christmas (if you were from a middle-class family).

Since launching, more than thirty million Baby-G watches have been sold across the globe. Although peaking in popularity in the mid to late 90s, the watches have crept back into the fashion fold thanks to associations with pop royalty like Rihanna and Lady Gaga.

Today, more than eighty different styles of Baby-G can be bought. Limited edition series made in collaboration with fashion designers, and associations with brand ambassadors from the music, skating and surfing worlds have given the brand new life, in a new decade, more than twenty years after its birth.

BUCKET HATS

Previously the domain of elderly fishermen and Gilligan from *Gilligan's Island*, the bucket hat was hot property in the 90s with both men and women.

Defying the traditional boundaries of fashion, the not especially flattering bucket hat was embraced by wildly different people in the 90s. Liam Gallagher hid behind a Kangol brand bucket hat, pubescent girls flipped their brims and accessorised with big flowers to be just like Blossom, and even supermodels like Naomi Campbell got in on the action by pairing a denim bucket hat with flawless hair and makeup.

Another 90s fashion trend that was arguably kicked off by rappers in the 80s, the bucket hat is also an extremely practical piece of headgear, keeping your head a sizzle-free zone in summer. This explains why, looking out onto festival crowds, most musicians in the 90s would have seen a sea of bucket hats. From psychedelic tie-dye to simple terry towelling, the ubiquitous bucket hat was *the* headwear of choice for music festival-goers in the decade.

By the 00s, the bucket hat's appeal began to wane when fedoras, Von Dutch caps and baker boy hats (a trio of cringe right there) muscled in on its territory. But proving that you can't keep a good hat down, bucket hats have recently staged a comeback with Rihanna doing her darndest to resurrect the trend by releasing her own line inspired by the 90s originals.

SNEAKERS

The influence that basketball had over sneaker styles and their popularity in the 90s cannot be overstated. Even though Air Jordan and Reebok Pump sneakers were first released in the 80s, their power and influence grew to epic proportions in the 90s.

First found on the feet of elite basketballers, these feature-packed shoes soon infiltrated suburbia, with all the coolest kids donning the latest release Nike Air Max or Air Jordan sneakers (while all the less fortunate could do nothing but look on with *extreme* envy). The sneakers were so valuable at the time that many teens feared walking home from school or the mall, in case their brand-new sneakers were stolen off their feet.

Decades later, we're seeing iconic Air Jordan re-releases, including the Air Jordan 12 'Flu Game' sneakers: the design worn by Michael Jordan in the 1997 final against the Utah Jazz where he played through dehydration, illness and exhaustion to secure a phenomenal 38 points. The original shoes were auctioned off for more than US$100,000, but these kinds of retro releases allow contemporary superfans to wear a little slice of history (at a more affordable price).

However, the 90s sneaker boom wasn't just for basketballers and jocks. At the other end of the sneaker spectrum, grunge fans laced up their trusty, festival-battered Converse All-Stars (when not in their Doc Martens of course). Vans were the footwear of choice for skaters, kids loved the razzle dazzle of LA Lights (those sneakers with a light built into the sole) and New Balance sneakers were a more expensive choice reserved for the types of people who could be bothered to clean their sneakers.

But beyond the cult labels and iconic brands, the bright, white, chunky trainers (often matched with high-waisted jeans) that ended up becoming the standard uniform of Jerry Seinfeld were a prevailing trend throughout the decade. Favoured by everyone from suburban dads, to the gang from *Beverly Hills 90210*, the 'mom jeans' and white sneakers combo remains a truly iconic 90s look.

THAT'S SO 90S!

White Men Can't Jump

Do you want to see some sweet early-90s basketball sneakers in action? The 1992 classic *White Men Can't Jump* is a parade of the decade's best kicks on the feet of Wesley Snipes, Woody Harrelson and an ensemble cast that includes ex-NBA stars. Notable styles include Nike Air Command Force, Nike Air Flight Lite and the Air Jordan VI which was packed with features like a heel tab inspired by Michael Jordan's Porsche, translucent soles and a two-hole pull on the tongue for easy entry.

SUPERMODELS

Twiggy and Jean Shrimpton ruled the 60s; Jerry Hall, Iman and Deborah Hutton had a good run in the 70s; and Brooke Shields and Cheryl Tiegs were the faces of the 80s. But in the 90s, a formidable crop of genetically blessed super-humans made their mark on the world while laughing all the way to the bank.

From runways to billboards, magazine covers and video clips, supermodels were everywhere in the 90s. There were the massive names like Naomi Campbell, Christy Turlington, Cindy Crawford, Linda Evangelista and Claudia Schiffer (known as 'The Big Five'), but there was also Helena Christensen, Niki Taylor, Karen Mulder, Stephanie Seymour, Kate Moss (famous for making 'heroin chic' a thing) and Tatjana Patitz (often referred to as the 'forgotten supermodel').

This new echelon of models were able to command huge fees – with Linda Evangelista famously saying (and later retracting) that she didn't get out of bed for anything less than $10,000 – and luxury labels such as Guess, Versace, Calvin Klein, Yves Saint Laurent and Chanel were happy to throw millions at supermodels.

Pop icon George Michael had a particular thing for supermodels, with the music video for 'Freedom! '90' featuring a stacked deck of early-90s legends (Christy, Cindy, Naomi, Linda and Tatjana) and 'Too Funky' featuring Eva Herzigova, Tyra Banks, Emma Balfour and more. Supermodels regularly popped up in film clips, with Stephanie Seymour appearing in the Guns N' Roses 'November Rain' clip and a topless Helena Christensen on the beach in Chris Isaak's 'Wicked Game' video.

While 90s supermodels reinforced unrealistic beauty standards and glorified luxury consumer goods most of the population couldn't afford (which wasn't exactly anything new); and they may have enjoyed fame and fortune, travelled the world, influenced pop culture and made a mint in the process, but they also probably missed out on a decade of eating bread guilt-free, so maybe the joke is on them?

MUSIC

Buying CDs in music stores, listening to albums in full, and lining up in person to buy concert tickets; being a music fan in the 90s required commitment, investment and staying power. Grunge gave a voice to a generation, hip-hop went mainstream, Britpop got serious airplay and power vocalists blasted the adult contemporary charts away. Jane's Addiction and Nine Inch Nails played at the very first Lollapalooza festival and Spike Jonze directed seminal music videos for the Beastie Boys, Björk, Weezer and Sonic Youth. With all-time greats like Prince, Madonna and Michael Jackson continuing to dominate the charts, the 90s grabbed the baton from the 80s and ran a personal best.

MICHAEL BOLTON

Sure, it was the decade of grunge, but let's not forget about the strides made in the adult contemporary category during the 90s. While teens were busy worshipping boy bands, rocking out to Seattle's finest or swearing up a storm rapping along to Tupac, their parents were slipping into something comfortable, pouring themselves a merlot and inserting the latest Michael Bolton disc into their CD player.

A regular on the music scene in the 70s and 80s, it wasn't until the early 90s that the husky-voiced hunk with one of the greatest hairstyles of the decade became a household name. Reinvigorating the easy-listening genre with impassioned hits like 'How Can We Be Lovers', 'Said I Loved You … But I Lied' and 'Can I Touch You … There?', Bolton has sold more than 75 million records over the course of his career, with the 90s accounting for a large portion of those sales.

Featured in *People* magazine's Sexiest Man Alive issue multiple times, the man with the golden mane was much more than a pretty-faced crooner your mother had fantasies about. Working with everyone from Bob Dylan to Pavarotti, Bolton won multiple Grammy Awards, yet managed to keep his feet firmly on the ground despite his sex-symbol status. Using his profile to set up a charity in support of at-risk women and children, Michael Bolton's heart has proven to be as big as his hair.

Bolton's choice to cut his trademark flowing mullet in 1997 not only brought an end to his signature look but also marked a new phase in his career. Some believe that his cascading blond waves held the key to his success, and while it's true that his post-mullet albums haven't had the same impact as the ones he released when in full mullet mode, Bolton's staying power and work ethic ensures he still sells out shows from Bournemouth to Biloxi.

MARIAH CAREY

No matter what style of music you were into in the 90s, if you had functioning ears there's no way you'd have made it through the decade without hearing Mariah Carey's voice skipping through five octaves with ease.

Influenced by gospel, soul and R&B, Mariah Carey dominated the 90s like no other recording artist, releasing seven platinum albums in the decade: *Mariah Carey* in 1990, *Emotions* in 1991, *Music Box* in 1993, *Merry Christmas* in 1994, *Daydream* in 1995, *Butterfly* in 1997 and *Rainbow* in 1999.

An unexpected sleeper hit, *Merry Christmas* has become one of the highest selling Christmas albums of all time, joining influential artists like Elvis Presley, Bing Crosby and Kenny G. Featuring songs like 'All I Want for Christmas is You' and 'Santa Claus Is Comin' to Town', the sickly sweet album was a runaway success, even though critics were scathing of Mariah's contribution to the festive-album canon.

If you're in doubt about just how popular Mariah's Christmas album is then consider the fact that in 2017 'All I Want for Christmas Is You' hit Billboard's Top 10, a whopping twenty-three years after its release. The song is officially no longer a song but a possessed entity, rising from slumber every December to decimate holiday song records and terrorise retail staff with non-stop rotation all throughout the shopping season.

After the golden years of the 90s, Mariah released fewer hits and many more misses (her so-bad-it's-good 2001 film *Glitter* was a low point). Yet despite her flops, Mimi can still lay claim to eighteen number ones on the Billboard Hot 100, thirty-four Grammy Award nominations, more than 200 million albums sold and a cool half-a-billion bucks in the bank.

CELINE DION

The 90s saw adult contemporary music unabashedly embracing overblown power ballads filled with saccharine lyrics. While plenty of artists dreamed of dominating the genre, no one did it quite like Celine Dion.

Already an outright star in her homeland of Canada, it was in the 90s that Queen Celine conquered the rest of the world. With a string of successful French-language albums behind her, Dion's first English-language album debuted in 1990. By the end of the decade she would have released five more albums, won five Grammy Awards, performed at the Academy Awards ceremony and earned an obscene amount of cash.

Even though Celine possesses one hell of a voice and was responsible for hit after hit, many critics were unimpressed with the composition of her songs and her overly dramatic shtick. But it's this unashamed love of drama, sense of theatre and rejection of subtlety that makes Celine, Celine. Nuance? Pffft. This is the woman whose 1994 wedding was broadcast live on Canadian television.

Aside from *that* theme song from *that* movie, one of Dion's biggest legacies has to be her film clips from the 90s. Made in the era where many music videos played like mini-movies, complete with involved plotlines, celebrity guest stars and gnarly special effects, many of Dion's singles were accompanied by epic, bodice-ripping film clips featuring story arcs worthy of a Mills & Boon page-turner. Majestic castles, ghost lovers, halls of mirrors, palm-reading beaus, lightning strikes, fireballs and heavy use of smoke and wind machines … they just don't make 'em like they used to.

ALANIS MORISSETTE

In the mid-90s, a relatively unknown Canadian barely into her twenties mastered the art of the fierce-as-hell break-up song, providing a much-needed rage outlet for a generation of women feeling the pain of being dumped, cheated on, used or duped by men.

Released in 1995, *Jagged Little Pill* reminded women that they were allowed to unleash their strong opinions. It also resulted in countless people questioning the meaning of the word 'ironic' and got plenty of teens into trouble with their parents for screaming verbal ice-picks laden with swear words and sexual references.

The album was a huge commercial success, resulting in several chart-topping singles including 'You Oughta Know', 'Ironic' and 'Hand in My Pocket'. It also earned Morissette an Album of the Year nod at the Grammy Awards and coveted number one status in the United States, the United Kingdom, Canada, Australia, New Zealand, Sweden and beyond. Accolades aside, her 'Head Over Feet' track popularised the term 'friend with benefits', a lasting pop-culture legacy if ever there was one.

An unapologetic song loaded with suggestive lyrics, 'You Oughta Know' was always going to raise eyebrows, but when the world discovered that Alanis once dated actor Dave Coulier, the rumour mill went into overdrive. Could 'You Oughta Know' really be about Uncle Joey from *Full House*? Please let it be about Uncle Joey from *Full House*! Dave divulged that the song *was* written about him, but retracted the comment years later.

Today, Morissette maintains a successful acting career (who can forget her turn as God in Kevin Smith's *Dogma*?) and continues to release successful records. Alanis gave fed-up women a voice and managed to slip a lyric asking if she would 'go down on you in a theatre'? into a mainstream song – a legendary feat for the mid-90s (even if radio stations censored it).

90s CROSSOVER ALERT!

'You Oughta Know' also features Red Hot Chili Peppers' Flea on bass and Dave Navarro on guitar.

SPICE GIRLS

Just when we thought that the 90s was going to be all about grunge, Britpop and hip-hop, the Spice Girls zig-a-zig-ahhhhed into our lives and broke almost all the records.

Love 'em or loathe 'em, no other girl group had a greater impact on pop culture in the 90s than the Spice Girls. Comprising Emma Bunton, Victoria Adams (now Beckham), Geri Halliwell, Melanie Brown and Melanie Chisholm as Baby, Posh, Ginger, Scary and Sporty Spices respectively – the Spice Girls are the biggest selling girl group of all time, with more than 85 million records sold worldwide.

From Ginger Spice's Union Jack mini-dress to Mel C's retro tracksuits, the Spice Girls influenced the fashion world immensely, but their impact didn't end there. With their catchy girl-power lyrics, brash personalities and easily-replicated dance moves, the Spice Girls were a generation's unapologetically loud pop-feminist role models.

While *Spice World* the movie could be seen cynical as a cash grab, the fans lapped it up and *VICE* has since described it as a 'deranged, postmodern masterpiece'. The film is jam-packed with celebrity cameos. Look closely and you'll see Elvis Costello, Meat Loaf, Jennifer Saunders, Elton John, Roger Moore, Stephen Fry and Bob Geldof in the film (Gary Glitter ended up on the cutting room floor after being nailed on sexual assault charges after production).

Nominated for more than ten Golden Raspberry Awards, legendary American film critic Roger Ebert could only give *Spice World* half a star, such was his disgust at the film. Despite being savaged by critics, the film made serious cash due to the huge legions of young women who would have followed the Girl Power brigade into a war if they were asked (90s fandom was a serious business).

Whether or not you're a fan, no one can argue with the fact that the Spice Girls released a string of bona fide pop classics – chances are you still know most of the lyrics to 'Wannabe' (including the part where Mel B raps) and all of the dance moves to 'Stop'.

JANET JACKSON

Michael, the King of Pop, sure had a lot of big moments in the 90s, but it was also the decade that his sister Janet managed to step out from the Jackson Family shadow to emerge as a superstar in her own right.

Starting the decade with a blockbuster ten-month world tour in support of her 1989 album *Rhythm Nation*, Janet's career went from strength to strength, consolidating her place in pop recording history. Performing more than one hundred shows across the United States, Canada, Europe and Japan, Janet spent most of 1990 playing stadium shows for thousands of adoring fans.

Jackson then backed it up with *janet.* in 1993. Stacked with radio-friendly hits, the album resulted in not one, not two, but *six* top ten hits on the US charts including the huge track 'That's the Way Love Goes'. An album that revealed a more intimate side to the artist, *janet.* went on to sell a phenomenal fourteen-million copies worldwide.

Touring in support of *janet.*, Jackson went on to endure a gruelling tour schedule

that spanned from late 1993 to the middle of 1995. *Poetic Justice* was also released in 1993 – a film featuring a modern-day love story played out by Janet and 90s rap legend Tupac.

After experiencing an emotional breakdown caused by unresolved childhood trauma and a punishing work schedule, Janet took time out in the middle of the decade, only to re-emerge with a daring concept album that explored everything from BDSM to bisexuality.

Proving that you can't keep a good woman down, 1997's *The Velvet Rope* revealed yet another layer of Janet to the world. Considered a more introspective offering loaded with eroticism, *The Velvet Rope* sold more than ten million copies worldwide. Just like the artist herself, the hit single 'Together Again' had incredible longevity, spending an astounding twenty-six weeks on the Billboard Hot 100 chart.

Selling out stadiums, releasing two acclaimed albums and more than ten hit singles – the 90s belonged to Janet.

RADIOHEAD

There are bands that fit neatly into boxes. And then there's Radiohead. Not grunge. Not Britpop. A band made up of males but definitely not a boy band … Radiohead released a trio of albums in the 90s which allowed them to carve out a niche of their own.

First came *Pablo Honey* in 1993, with breakthrough track 'Creep' putting the band on Britain's radar. Then came *The Bends* in 1995, continuing the guitar-rock tradition, albeit with more thoughtful, intelligent lyrics than most of their contemporaries. The final album of the 90s trifecta was a departure from the previous two and a bold step in a new, experimental direction for the band.

Recorded at the probably-haunted St Catherine's Court estate in Somerset, England, *OK Computer* converted a whole new wave of listeners around the world to Radiohead fandom for life.

Released in June 1997, *OK Computer* was no ordinary album. An esoteric, cerebral offering that confounded record label executives. It was less of an album packed with radio-friendly hits and more of a conceptual opus full of tracks that get better and better with every listen.

Described by *Rolling Stone* as a 'Rhapsody in Gloom', *OK Computer* featured songs about plane crashes and aliens, a heartbreaking dirge crafted for *Romeo + Juliet* and an unsettling monologue from a depressed robot.

Even though the album was penned by a man fatigued by an unrelenting tour schedule, the album's conversations about consumerism and the impact of technology on society has been accepted as a prophetic warning of things to come. Indeed, much of what is put forward on the album feels strangely familiar. If anything, even more of us are now still striving to be fitter, happier, more productive …

90s CROSSOVER ALERT

At the time they were recording *OK Computer*, St Catherine's Court estate was owned by Jane Seymour – a 90s icon in her own right as the star of *Dr. Quinn, Medicine Woman*.

THAT'S SO 90S!

Alternative rock

Alternative music had huge appeal in the 90s, as listeners turned away from the mainstream to embrace a key cohort of grunge and indie acts like Smashing Pumpkins, Pearl Jam, Soundgarden, Alice in Chains, Mudhoney, Temple of the Dog, L7, Hole and Babes in Toyland. The genre originally referred to music springing from independent, underground record labels – an alternative to those 'sell-out' bands who signed recording contracts for like, money. Of course all of this music then became the new mainstream, prompting many an argument about that Gen-X Holy Grail, 'authenticity', and proving that there were just as many hipsters in the 90s as there are now, they just wore more flannel.

OASIS

Following in the footsteps of The Beatles (and famously proclaiming they were bigger than The Beatles, and if the Beatles were bigger than Jesus, well …), a bunch of pasty-skinned, working-class lads from the United Kingdom rose up to become one of the biggest bands of the 90s – making hard drinking, chain smoking, shit talking and not giving a toss what other people think cool again.

Fronted by two mercurial brothers from Manchester, Oasis led the charge in the rise of Britpop. With the release of two hit albums in the mid-90s, Oasis offered an alternative look to the grunge trend that was dominating the music scene at the time.

Noel and Liam Gallagher's distinct aesthetic spawned a wave of lookalikes sporting shaggy haircuts, sideburns, John Lennon glasses and bucket hats. Fashion trends aside, Oasis had so much influence because their music was very, very good.

Released in 1994, their debut album *Definitely Maybe* was a runaway success in the UK, the United States and beyond, selling millions worldwide. The 1995 release *(What's the Story) Morning Glory?* is packed with dead-set classics like 'Wonderwall' and 'Some Might Say'. Oasis' second album remains one of the UK's fastest-selling albums of all time and an enduring favourite on the karaoke circuit.

The pulling power of Oasis in the 90s is best demonstrated by the open-air concerts the band played at Knebworth House in 1996. An astounding 2.5 million people (four per cent of Britain's population!) applied for tickets with a lucky 250,000 seeing Oasis play over two days.

Of course, breaking records, raking in the cash, and knowing that millions of people are clamouring to see you play was always going to stoke the self-destructive nature of the Gallaghers. From feuding with Blur, to taking pot shots at Radiohead and warring with each other, Oasis's heyday slowly gave way to an era characterised by bitter fights, nasty insults and petty wars of words that still rage on Twitter decades later.

It's interesting that the band that gave us 'Don't Look Back in Anger' can't seem to take their own advice, but that's life, innit?

RAGE AGAINST
the Machine

Once upon a time in the 90s, before people claimed to be activists because they signed an online petition or once tweeted a senator, a group of musicians from LA rewrote the rules on just how far recording artists can go in the name of a political cause.

Formed in Los Angeles in 1991, Rage Against the Machine (RATM) were much more than a rock/metal/hip-hop group out to sell a few records. Comprising Zack de la Rocha on vocals, Tom Morello on guitar, Tim Commerford on bass and vocals and Brad Wilk on drums, RATM were known for delivering bruising live performances that united audiences in hatred against oppression and injustice.

Forget sitting on the fence or carefully hiding your political opinion to not make waves with fans, as the band name suggests, Rage Against the Machine were all about making overtly political statements. Characterised by savage lyrics teamed with furious vocals and bombastic bass lines, RATM released songs that were anti-war, anti-corruption, anti-government and anti–corporate America.

Never happy to just pay lip service to causes, band members aggressively railed against authority by protesting immigration laws, sweatshop working conditions, capital punishment, Guantanamo Bay and the military–industrial complex.

From standing on stage naked with duct tape over their mouths at Lollapalooza in 1993 to getting kicked off *Saturday Night Live* for attempting to fly the American flag upside down (the signal of a nation in distress), RATM galvanised audiences to think about power, corruption, war and inequality.

Politics aside, if you were an angry teen sick of being told what to do by your parents, teachers or the cops, 'Killing in the Name Of' provided one of the greatest, most cathartic sweary scream-alongs ever written, allowing a whole generation to vent their pent-up frustrations and scare the hell out of their parents.

THAT'S SO 90S!

Riot Grrrls

The Riot Grrrl movement had been raising hell long before the Spice Girls found a way to cash in on female empowerment. Starting in Olympia, Washington, then spreading throughout the Pacific Northwest and to the rest of the world, the underground feminist movement was spearheaded by female-led punk outfits that were proudly political and absolutely done with the patriarchy. Bands such as Bikini Kill, Bratmobile, Calamity Jane and Excuse 17 were about much more than music, they were a part of a grassroots movement that tackled everything from racism to homophobia, and that drunk dude that likes to mansplain the origins of punk to all the little ladies at gigs.

NIRVANA

A band that came to define a generation and become the poster children for the Seattle grunge scene, there was nothing cooler than Nirvana in the early 90s.

Releasing only three albums (*Bleach*, *Nevermind* and *In Utero*), Kurt Cobain, Krist Novoselic and a very young Dave Grohl were the anaemic royalty early-90s teens worshipped with cult-like reverence.

Lyrics infused with teen angst, Gen-X cynicism and an overwhelming sense of gloom helped Nirvana connect with millions of young people who were distrustful of adults, teachers, the government and anything that reeked of authority or effort.

With roots in punk, Nirvana's colossal tunes featuring heavy riffs, blistering drums and dark, somewhat prophetic lyrics has seen the band's influence extend far beyond the 90s. Wearing cardigans, Converse, striped shirts, ripped jeans and a general air of chronic dissatisfaction, Kurt Cobain was the spirit animal of long-haired, disaffected teens the world over who began dressing like him in the 90s and never really stopped.

Cobain's shocking death by suicide in April 1994 caused waves of grief to reverberate around the world. The band's *MTV Unplugged in New York* album, released seven months after Cobain's death, went straight to number one, garnering a Grammy for Best Alternative Music Album. It's still considered one of the greatest live albums ever produced.

As is often the case with tragedy, Cobain's death cemented Nirvana's place as one of the most influential bands of all time. Kurt's entry into the '27 Club' ensured the band remained forever young. Nirvana fans may have lost a legend, but they also never had to see their hero go down the demoralising path of releasing substandard albums, playing residencies in Las Vegas or ending up as a guest judge on *The X Factor*.

Nirvana are forever frozen in time as a relic of another time – a time when fans bought albums on tape and CD, and slept outside in the rain lining up for concert tickets. It's for this reason that there will never be another Nirvana. The world has changed, but Nirvana will always remain the same.

GREEN DAY

Offering an alternative to every other sound on the music scene in the early 90s, three tattooed dudes from Oakland, California, emerged to give a voice to a generation of demotivated, frustrated, responsibility-shirkers, trapped in the ennui of teenagerdom.

With Billie Joe Armstrong on guitar and vocals, Mike Dirnt on bass and Tré Cool on drums, Green Day weren't grunge, shoegaze, pop, rock, thrash or metal. Instead they offered an American brand of (mostly) radio-friendly, high-energy punk.

Releasing a string of hit albums – *39/ Smooth* in 1990, *Kerplunk* in 1991, *Dookie* in 1994, *Insomniac* in 1995 and *Nimrod* in 1997 – Green Day were a constant companion to anyone feeling on the outer of society.

With references to masturbation, anxiety, drug use, boredom, self-loathing and chronic grottiness, Green Day's lyrics tapped into the seemingly endless tedium of being a teen. Being on the cusp of adulthood presents a unique set of challenges (oh the horror of dealing with zits, exams, homework, parents and forced participation in ball sports). For many, Green Day was the answer.

Accused by some of commercialising a watered-down, vanilla version of punk, Green Day might not have endeared themselves to the likes of pioneering punk performers such as Sex Pistols' front man Johnny Rotten, but they sure were appreciated by millions of fans in the 90s.

Green Day's memorable mud fight with fans at Woodstock '94 has gone down in history as one of the loosest festival sets ever performed. Mud was slung, instruments were ruined and teeth were lost; it's hard to imagine anything like that going down at a modern-day Coachella set.

THAT'S SO 90S!

Boy bands

While Green Day were slinging mud and Oasis were busy abusing their bodies, fighting with rivals and indulging in other twat behaviour, clusters of clean-cut, well-behaved, non-threatening young men were forming radio-friendly groups of their own. Boy bands such as Backstreet Boys, Take That, NSYNC, Boyzone and Boyz II Men may not have grabbed the headlines like those bands behaving badly, but they sure did pack out suburban malls and occupy serious real estate on bedroom walls, lockers and school diaries around the world.

BOOKS

A decade perfect for distraction-free reading produced a catalogue of hugely influential books. From chick-lit to self-help, violent thrillers, feminist manifestos and R-rated celebrity vanity projects masquerading as art, the 90s gave readers many reasons to head to the local bookstore or library.

Released in 1992 as a companion piece to her *Erotica* album, Madonna's risqué coffee table book caused quite a stir. While Madonna was no stranger to controversy, never before had a mainstream artist pushed the envelope so far as to release an X-Rated book filled with graphic images of bondage, masturbation and threesomes.

Some viewed the book as nothing more than pornography (it was banned in Japan), but despite the scandal and furore that the book invoked, Madonna's star power ensured the tome ended up a *New York Times* Best Seller.

With provocative images of Isabella Rossellini, Naomi Campbell and Madonna's beau-of-the-minute Vanilla Ice also sandwiched between the book's metal covers, *Sex* was always destined to capture the attention of fans who wanted to own a slice of publishing history.

While not remembered as high art, the book did an excellent job of generating publicity for *Erotica* and keeping Madonna in the headlines. In a masterstroke that showed Madonna's marketing genius and unashamed self-promotion, this book proves that sex really does sell.

90s TREND ALERT!

Madonna's book wasn't her only controversial move in the 90s. In 1990, her raunchy video for 'Justify My Love' was banned from MTV. In 1991, Toronto authorities threatened to shut down her *Blond Ambition* show due to her simulating masturbation on stage. And in 1994, she swore her way through a memorable appearance on the *Late Show with David Letterman*. The episode become one of the most censored in American talk-show history.

THE BEAUTY MYTH

Published in 1990, Naomi Wolf's seminal feminist manifesto was hyped as a provocative look at how women are undermined by unrealistic beauty ideals perpetuated by a patriarchal society that trains men to evaluate women based on their appearance.

Looking at how women around the world are pressured to lose weight, undertake cosmetic surgery, wear makeup, get a tan, slather on anti-ageing creams, shave their legs and dye their hair, *The Beauty Myth* takes aim at the unrealistic expectations propagated by advertisers, women's magazines and fashion houses.

A text that found its way onto college curriculums and sparked the so-called third-wave feminist movement, *The Beauty Myth: How Images of Beauty Are Used Against Women* shows contemporary readers that concerns about objectification of women aren't really anything new. Depressingly enough, the issues highlighted in the book are still prevalent, if not worse than they were in the 90s.

Written pre–social media, some of the content in the book may now read as a little dated, but replace women's magazines with social media, supermodels with Instagram influencers and 90s-era porn with contemporary porn, and the message is still on target.

While many have pointed out that Wolf's work focuses on the experiences of white, middle-class, privileged women, *The Beauty Myth* lit a fire under many women who started calling bullshit on the whole waxing, shaving, plucking, tanning and dieting caper.

FIGHT CLUB

Chuck Palahniuk's 1996 debut satiric novel introduced a generation of readers to a brutal, warped world and gained a cult following in the process.

Exploring themes like masculinity, capitalism and consumerist culture, *Fight Club* forced readers to question everything about the society they lived in, which no doubt resulted in a fair few existential crises.

As the unnamed, insomnia-plagued narrator goes searching for answers, he meets Tyler Durden, a sociopath who (among other things) steals human fat from liposuction clinics to make into soap. Tyler introduces the narrator to Fight Club, a secret club where men come together, take off their shoes and shirt and engage in bare-knuckle, one-on-one fights.

Lauded for its inventive approach, blistering commentary on the state of society and well-hidden twist ending, *Fight Club*'s loyal following only grew with the release of the 1999 David Fincher film starring Brad Pitt and Edward Norton.

Much more than a story about a bunch of bros fighting, *Fight Club* inspired a generation to take control of their lives (although, perhaps not to the extreme, psychopathic level of Tyler Durden).

Railing against advertising, corporations, dead-end jobs, New Age spirituality, Hollywood movies (ironically) and all the trappings of modern society that keep us running on the hamster wheel, the messages in *Fight Club* are every bit as applicable today as they were when the book was first published. If anything, *Fight Club* is more relevant now than ever before.

90s TRIVIA ALERT!

Chuck Palahniuk has taken credit for coining the term 'snowflake', used to describe easily offended, precious people. The term appears in both the book and the film.

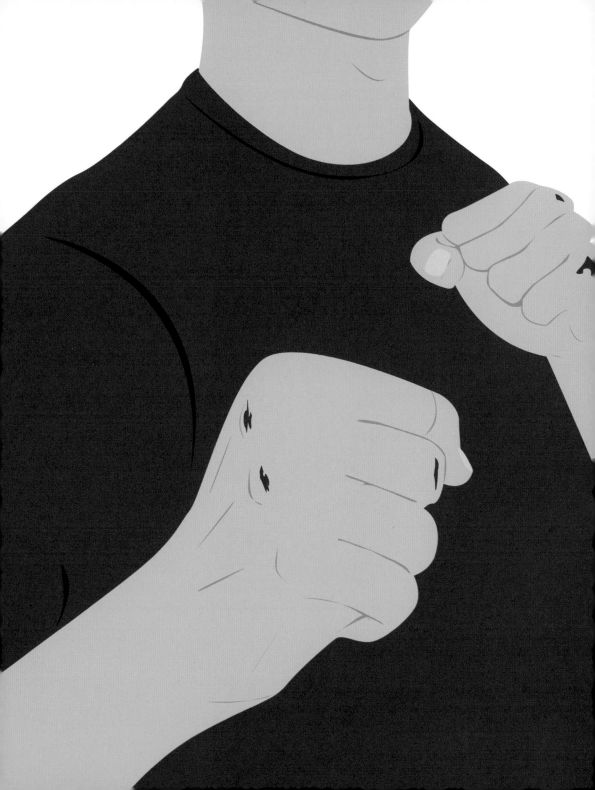

GENERATION X:

Tales for an Accelerated Culture

Published in 1991, Douglas Coupland's ground-breaking missive on a generation that he believed to be overlooked and mischaracterised ended up coining a term that is still used today, and landing him in a situation he wasn't quite comfortable with.

Popularising the label 'Generation X' to describe the post–Baby Boomer generation born during and after the early 1960s, Coupland's book generated a surge in interest in the generation that he belonged to and was seeking to characterise in the book.

Focusing on the lives of a group of twenty-somethings living in the suburban sprawl of inland California, this witty, pop culture–drenched book rails against consumerism, meaningless work, career climbing and all the expectations placed on young people to 'succeed'.

Chapter names like 'I Am Not a Target Market', 'Shopping is Not Creating', 'Purchased Experiences Don't Count' and 'Adventure Without Risk is Disneyland' give you a pretty good idea of the book's themes.

While many writers would have exploited this popularity for financial gain, Coupland stubbornly refused to capitalise on his fame as the author of a generation-defining book that skewers commercialism. After all, 'selling out' was the worst crime an artist could commit in the 90s.

Lamenting that the term 'Generation X' has been co-opted by marketers and the media ever since his book hit the shelves, Coupland resisted the temptation to piggyback off the book's success, famously refusing to become a spokesperson for the generation, even turning down work to create ads for the Gap clothing company. Just like a true Gen-Xer would.

THE BEACH

This travel-thriller novel by Alex Garland was released in 1996 and soon became a cult hit among the cohort of dreadlocked, fisherman's pants–wearing backpackers who descended on South East Asia in the late 90s.

Centring on the experiences of white, middle-class European backpackers embarking on a quest to a secret island in Thailand, this novel has it all. Love triangles, power struggles, shark attacks, a secret society, drug crops, hallucinations and descents into madness, *The Beach* is a rollicking read from beginning to end.

A best seller that was turned into a hit movie directed by Danny Boyle and starring 90s man-of-the-moment Leonardo DiCaprio, *The Beach* walks the line between cautionary tale and page-turning thriller and readers lapped it up.

Well-thumbed copies of *The Beach* can still be found lurking everywhere around the globe – in hostel libraries, in thrift stores, and in bars and cafes on Bangkok's Khao San Road (the backpacker hub which features in the beginning of the book).

If you want to know what travel was like before Skype, Instagram, iPhones, laptops, and selfie sticks came along, then the closest you'll get is reading *The Beach*.

90s TRIVIA ALERT!

Author Alex Garland is now a successful Hollywood player. He penned *28 Days Later* and *Sunshine* for Danny Boyle and has recently turned his hand to directing with *Ex Machina* and *Annihilation*.

MEN ARE FROM MARS,

Women Are From Venus

Published in 1992, relationship counsellor John Gray's first foray into self-help publishing was less of a flash-in-the-pan best seller and more of a blueprint for building an empire and making a truckload of money.

Reportedly one of the decade's highest-selling books, in the 90s *Men Are From Mars, Women Are From Venus* could be found on millions of bookshelves and bedside tables around the world. From disgruntled housewives looking for answers, to newly divorced men hoping to understand what the hell went wrong, Gray took a whole lot of generalisations about gender, packaged them up as the answer to everyone's relationship problems and laughed all the way to the bank.

Spawning a talk-show series, stage show, various seminars and events, international tours, retreats, and author appearances on *Oprah* and *The Phil Donahue Show*, few adults would have got through the 90s without having encountered the *Men Are From Mars, Women Are From Venus* brand in some shape or form.

Squeezing every last dollar out of the idea, Gray has gone on to pen a mind-boggling number of spin-off books including but not limited to: *Mars and Venus in Love, Mars and Venus in the Bedroom, Mars and Venus on a Date, Mars and Venus Starting Over, Mars and Venus: 365 Ways to Keep Passion Alive, Mars and Venus in the Workplace, Why Mars and Venus Collide* and *The Mars and Venus Diet and Exercise Solution*.

With so many sequels, *Men Are From Mars, Women Are From Venus* is pretty much *The Fast and the Furious* of the book world, but with one hundred per cent less Vin Diesel.

PROZAC NATION

First published in 1994, *Prozac Nation: Young and Depressed in America: A Memoir* tapped into the slacker generation's belief that, since everything is so screwed up beyond repair, why even bother trying?

Written by American journalist Elizabeth Wurtzel, the candid memoir catalogues years of severe depressive episodes characterised by suicide attempts, self-harm, drug use, hospitalisation, break-ups, confrontation with family and, as the title suggests, the prescription anti-depressant marketed under the name Prozac.

Despite Wurtzel's raw writing style being panned by many reviewers and the book dismissed by critics as a self-indulgent whinge-fest, many readers connected with Wurtzel's warts-and-all mental health memoir. With many Generation X teens witnessing their parents' ugly divorces, *Prozac Nation*'s honest exploration of the universal themes of teen angst and family separation really hit a nerve with a generation of young people who felt alienated from their parents and let down by society.

Going on to become a best seller, for a time there *Prozac Nation* was *the* book read by young people on college campuses and school buses all over the world. Eventually adapted into a ho-hum movie starring Christina Ricci in 2001, *Prozac Nation* may not be remembered for being a great book, but its influence on the memoir genre and sway with readers can't be denied.

HIGH FIDELITY

The closest thing male readers had to the guy equivalent of chick-lit, Nick Hornby's *High Fidelity* hit bookstores in 1995 and became an instant success.

Focusing on the life of commitment-phobic, mid-thirties, record shop–owner and compulsive list-maker Rob Fleming, many readers saw elements of themselves in the book's highly relatable protagonist who is staring down some sort of mid-life crisis after yet another relationship break-up. Turning to music to get him through the hard times, Rob reflects on his previous relationships while cataloguing the songs and albums that have influenced his life.

An instant classic that highlights many pop-cultural hallmarks of the 90s, *High Fidelity* is a funny, endearing novel for music aficionados and anyone who has ever felt like they are muddling their way through life. Written before big chains and then music streaming sent record stores into decline, the book is all about albums, mix tapes, favourites lists and long, hypothetical conversations you have with others (and yourself) about what music you'd need to take with you when marooned on a deserted island.

Adapted into a not-bad-at-all film starring John Cusack, *High Fidelity* brilliantly captures what now looks like a thoroughly old-fashioned aesthetic. Viewed through modern eyes, *High Fidelity* will make you wistful for simpler times, when the only way you could get music was to buy an album and people could still make a living running a second-hand record store.

1. Alison Ashworth
2. Penny Hardwick

TOP 5

MOST MEMORABLE SPLIT-UPS

3. Jackie Allen
4. Charlie Nicholson
5. Sarah Kendrew

AMERICAN PSYCHO

As far as controversial books go, *American Psycho* is up there with Salman Rushdie's *The Satanic Verses*.

First published in 1991, *American Psycho* was written in an era when the world was groggily waking up from a collective hangover induced by the excesses of 1980s Wall Street. Greed was no longer good in the 90s and rampant consumerism was becoming frowned upon.

So how does a young author demonstrate the ills of unchecked capitalism? With a satiric, darkly humorous novel featuring an investment banker with psychopathic tendencies who murders children, tortures animals, blinds a homeless man, eats the flesh of women and does something so abhorrent with a rat that some readers still haven't recovered more than twenty-five years after picking up the book.

Written off by many critics as nothing more than a nasty, sensationalist snuff-novel, *American Psycho* drew controversy from all corners upon its release. Author Bret Easton Ellis reportedly received death threats, many bookstores refused to stock the book and some countries gave the book an R rating, which meant buyers had to be over eighteen to buy the plastic-wrapped book.

Interspersed between grotesquely graphic descriptions of violent murder, torture and cannibalism, the book is loaded with pop-culture diatribes (Donald Trump even gets a mention) as well as wry observations on everyday life. It's this experimental approach to fiction that made Bret Easton Ellis a household name. That, and the references to cannibalism.

Despite leaving a generation of book-lovers desperately wishing they could unread what they'd just read, *American Psycho* went on to be adapted into a movie starring Christian Bale and, strangely enough, a Broadway musical. With lines like: 'There's no use in denying it: this has been a bad week. I've started drinking my own urine', it's easy to see why *American Psycho* has both fascinated and horrified the public since its release.

BRIDGET JONES'S
Diary

First published in 1996, *Bridget Jones's Diary* heralded the age of the highly entertaining chick-lit novel and provided author Helen Fielding with very healthy royalty cheques for decades to come.

Chronicling the life and times of a thirty-something British anti-heroine prone to smoking, drinking, swearing and sleeping with unsuitable men, *Bridget Jones's Diary* sold millions of copies and gave voice to a generation of women who had never seen their experiences reflected in popular culture before.

Every single, career woman who'd ever shagged their boss, struggled into restrictive shapewear or endured awkward dinner parties with smug married couples was finally being validated by an endearing character who bumbled through life with humour and honesty.

From loathing Bridget's lecherous boss Daniel, to crushing on *Pride and Prejudice*–inspired love interest Mark Darcy and secretly wishing Bridget's core group of friends were real people you could turn to during times of crisis, readers lapped up the crass, neurotic, laugh-out-loud diary entries that catalogued Bridget's often highly relatable life.

Originally published as a newspaper column, then a book, the Bridget Jones concept was turned into not one, not two, but three feature films starring Renee Zellweger, Hugh Grant and Colin Firth. While the franchise spans decades (the third book was published as late as 2013), the first two novels are like a time capsule for anyone who didn't get to experience London in the 1990s: a magical, mystical place where people kept diaries, smoked in pubs and hooked up without the help of Tinder.

GOOSEBUMPS

Before *Harry Potter*, *Twilight* and *The Hunger Games*, the legendary *Goosebumps* book series kept kids up late, reading way past their bedtime.

Hitting shelves in 1992, no one could have predicted how much of a runaway success *Goosebumps* would be. Releasing a mind-boggling sixty-two books in the decade, R.L. Stine's highly entertaining supernatural horror novels captured the attention of children around the globe thanks to translations into more than thirty languages.

Filled with ghosts, monsters, slime, menacing creatures and possessed dummies (who could forget Slappy the Dummy?), the *Goosebumps* series of books were nightmare fodder that somehow also managed to elicit laughs and chills at the same time – without completely terrifying readers. Devoid of violence, death, drug use and sex, the books were ultimately a pretty wholesome choice that parents embraced for tween readers.

It's been estimated that in the mid-90s, four million *Goosebumps* books were sold in one month alone. Overall, more than 400 million *Goosebumps* books have been sold worldwide, making R.L. Stine one of the world's wealthiest authors. A well-deserved reward for someone who essentially inspired a generation of reluctant readers to drop their video games and pick up a book instead.

A super-brand that has resulted in several spin-off book series, a television series, feature film, video games, stage play and musical, board games, comic books and tons of merchandise, *Goosebumps* is a powerful example of how kids really do love to read, especially when there are evil, creepy-as-hell, living, breathing, scarecrows involved.

IN THE NEWS

Court cases that drew higher television ratings than popular sitcoms, riots that brought a city to its knees, celebrities getting caught in compromising positions, menacing tech bugs that threatened life as we knew it and bizarre crimes that prove that fact is certainly stranger than fiction – the 90s news cycle was a hot mess full of drama, disaster and tragedy.

TONYA HARDING

& Nancy Kerrigan

When footage emerged of American champion figure skater Nancy Kerrigan clutching her leg and wailing 'Whyyyyy?' after being clubbed with a baton by a mysterious, leather-coated assailant at the US Figure Skating Championships in Detroit, the world was transfixed. Who would do such a thing to an elite athlete competing in a tournament? Turns out, associates of an elite athlete competing in the same tournament, that's who.

After a long rivalry on the ice, down-on-her-luck battler Tonya Harding and polished high achiever Nancy Kerrigan were competing in Detroit when Kerrigan was brutally attacked. Harding won, as Kerrigan was forced to withdraw due to her injury – but Kerrigan was still given a spot to compete in the upcoming Lillehammer Olympics alongside Harding.

Meanwhile, a police investigation into the incident continued and an almighty media circus unfolded – with tabloids and talk shows speculating on Harding's alleged involvement. An acquaintance of Harding's and her ex-husband were implicated in the crime and both were later charged.

Despite Harding's obvious connection to the assault, she still skated at the Lillehammer Olympics, but failed to win a medal after a strange, almost-karmic incident involving a broken shoelace. Kerrigan returned home with silver.

Harding never admitted to any involvement in the plot but eventually plead guilty to a minor charge. After being fined, stripped of her championship title and banned from competitive ice skating, Harding has dipped in and out of the spotlight since. She enjoyed a brief stint as a professional boxer, dabbled in automobile racing and appeared on *Dancing with the Stars* before re-emerging to promote 2017's Oscar-winning *I, Tonya*.

A modern American fable complete with twists and turns, heroes and villains, downfalls and redemption, the Kerrigan–Harding incident remains a cautionary tale about how unchecked ambition and a sense of entitlement can be rewarded with a Sufjan Stevens song and sympathetic Hollywood film being made in your honour.

LORENA

& John Wayne Bobbitt

When watching the contemporary news cycle (aka the never-ending trash fire), it can lead you to despair, 'What has become of the world?' Yet, it's important to remember that people in 1993 were thinking the same thing when they turned on the news to find that a woman had chopped off her husband's penis with a carving knife and thrown it into an empty field opposite a 7-Eleven in suburban Virginia.

While cutting off a man's penis may sound like an off-limits revenge fantasy to many women, Lorena Bobbitt turned that fantasy into reality. After allegedly enduring domestic abuse and rape at the hands of her husband, Lorena decided to go down the castration route in order to 'teach him a lesson'. Lorena obviously knew how to hit him where it hurt, as she also fled with his Nintendo Game Boy.

Hours later, police found John's penis, put it on ice (in a Big Bite hot dog container no less) and delivered it to the hospital for reattachment. The surgery was a success and John (and what became known as his 'Frankenpenis') went on to enjoy a brief career in the porn industry.

After the incident, both Lorena and John were charged with separate offences, but both were acquitted. Afterwards, Lorena mostly shunned the spotlight, choosing to go to college and set up a foundation for victims of domestic violence.

John, however, went on to be charged with multiple domestic violence and harassment offences against several women. Apart from starring in porn films, he also appeared as a knife thrower in the Jim Rose Circus and shamelessly courted the media (a *GQ* magazine article entitled 'Forrest Stump' remains a headline highlight).

So where are John and Lorena at with each other decades after the incident? A *Vanity Fair* profile published in 2018 reveals that John had sent a Facebook friend request to Lorena, which unsurprisingly remains unaccepted.

THE MURDER OF

JonBenét Ramsey

As one of the biggest unsolved crimes of the 90s, the murder of JonBenét Ramsey has been dissected by news networks, bloggers, column writers, true crime podcasters, crime network documentaries, *Dr. Phil* and countless Reddit threads.

It's a tragic fact that many children are murdered each day in America, however no other child-related crimes in the 90s received nearly as much attention and airplay as that of the murder of the Little Miss Colorado pageant winner.

When the six-year-old beauty queen was found dead in the basement of her family home in Boulder, Colorado, in December 1996, many people developed an unhealthy fascination with the case. A strange ransom note demanding $118,000 found in the family home pointed to a kidnapping-gone-wrong scenario, but suspicion was initially placed on JonBenét's parents. Talk shows and news networks went into meltdown as public speculation mounted, yet charges against the Ramseys never eventuated.

Over the years, the case has re-emerged from periodic slumber to get another run in the spotlight. The death of JonBenét's mother from cancer in 2006 thrust the case back into the news. In the same year, a man was arrested by police following a false confession (he was eventually released due to DNA at the scene not linking him to the crime). More recently, JonBenét's brother was tenuously linked to the crime by a salacious CBS docuseries, although no charges have been laid against him.

Despite years of investigations, news stories and digging by citizen sleuths, the unsolved case of who killed JonBenét Ramsey remains on the media merry-go-round, regularly being re-spun by tabloids, talk shows and telemovies.

DEARLY DEPARTED

If a cheesy Oscar's-style 'in memoriam' montage was put together for the 90s, it would elicit a lot of emotion. From plane crashes to drive-by shootings, fatal on-set mishaps and drug overdoses, the Grim Reaper reaped many highly influential celebrity souls during the 90s.

Teen heartthrob River Phoenix died of a drug overdose in LA's Viper Room on Halloween in 1993. In the same year, Brandon Lee (the son of legendary martial artist Bruce Lee) was shot and killed while filming *The Crow* after a production mix-up resulted in a live round ending up in the chamber of a prop gun.

Nirvana fans were devastated when voice of a generation Kurt Cobain died by suicide in 1994. Also in 1994, everyone's favourite cuddly comedian John Candy had his last laugh after suffering a heart attack while on location in Mexico. His last meal was reportedly spaghetti so we can assume he died a happy man.

Gifted rapper Tupac was famously shot to death in Las Vegas in 1996. His last words apparently whispered to a police officer were 'fuck you'. A year later, rapper The Notorious B.I.G. (aka Biggie Smalls) also died in a drive-by shooting in Los Angeles. His album *Life After Death* was released posthumously weeks after his passing.

In 1997, Italian fashion designer Gianni Versace was gunned down outside his Miami home by a thrill killer. The following month, the world collectively mourned the tragic death of Princess Diana who was killed in a car accident while being pursued by paparazzi.

Old Blue Eyes Frank Sinatra bowed out in 1998 and John F. Kennedy Jr. died in a plane crash off Martha's Vineyard in 1999, thus giving 'Kennedy Curse' conspiracy theorists plenty to speculate on.

GEORGE MICHAEL'S
Public Toilet Arrest

From DUIs to shoplifting (oh, Winona, why?), celebrities being arrested has been par for the course throughout the decades. After all, they are humans like us, and they make mistakes (but usually have funds to pay for a good lawyer).

But when a celebrity is arrested for something a little more salacious than the average run-of-the-mill crime, then the media goes into overdrive. Case in point: George Michael's arrest in 1998.

When news broke that George Michael had been arrested after being caught in a 'lewd act' in a public toilet located in a park in Beverly Hills, the world was fascinated. Readers wanted to know all the details of what the hell went on in that restroom.

Having just been caught with a man in a compromising position in a public place as part of an undercover police sting,

George Michael – who had until that time kept his sexuality private – was forcibly 'outed'. Ordered to pay a small fine and complete community service, George handled the event with grace and then came out swinging in true style.

Providing everyone with a masterclass on the right way to deal with a scandal, George Michael released the celebratory song 'Outside', accompanied by a cheeky film clip that referenced the event that led to his arrest. Considered a bold celebration of his sexuality, the film clip depicted George Michael in a police uniform dancing and singing to the words, 'Yesssss, I've been bad.'

Refusing to be shamed or demeaned, the British pop singer rose above the incident and even used it as a vehicle to get back into the charts. Bravo, George, bravo. Well played.

THE LA RIOTS

Whenever you start to feel that the world is turning to shit, imagine what people were thinking in 1992 when the LA Riots dominated news channels. Shocking world events may seem like a uniquely contemporary phenomenon, but the 90s had its fair share of dreadful moments.

After four police officers were acquitted of assault charges brought about after footage of black motorist Rodney King being brutally beaten was revealed to the public, LA exploded into violence. Frustrated at decades of police brutality, racism, inequality and a broken justice system, rioters in South Central Los Angeles took to the streets, destroying buildings, burning cars, looting shops and in some cases, beating civilians.

To put things into perspective, the riots were one of the biggest, most costly civil disturbances America has ever seen. Over five days, more than fifty people were killed and two thousand injured. More than a thousand buildings were damaged at an estimated cost of a billion US dollars.

Understandably, many residents and small business owners were fearful for their lives, as many parts of the city were in lockdown for days. The military and National Guard were called in to help restore order as the LAPD struggled to control the rioters despite night curfews being enacted.

Rodney King even made an impassioned plea to the city, saying: 'People, I just want to say, can we all get along? Can we get along? Can we stop making it horrible for the older people and the kids?' Yet stopping the rioting proved difficult when an oppressed population united in fury finally saw a chance to fight the system they'd long felt demoralised by.

Demonstrating the incredible power that video footage captured by ordinary people can have (King's beating was captured by a civilian), the devastating riots that shook LA for five days straight was in many ways the beginning of 'citizen journalism' and a prequel to the Black Lives Matter movement. Now, even more than ever, the LA Riots matter.

HUGH GRANT

& Divine Brown Get Busted

In the age before TMZ and Twitter, juicy sex scandals were the realm of tabloid newspapers and trashy magazines. Editors preyed on celebrities' mistakes, knowing that their publications would shift serious units any time a celeb got caught in a compromising position. Thankfully for them, in the 90s, celebrities gave them plenty to work with.

In 1995, Hugh Grant handed the tabloids the ultimate gift. In Hollywood to promote rom-com *Nine Months*, Grant was busted by police off Sunset Boulevard after he was discovered in his white BMW convertible with sex worker Divine Brown.

Looking mawkishly at the camera, shoulders hunched in a striped polo shirt, Hugh's infamous mugshot was circulated far and wide, appearing in newspapers, magazines and on the nightly television news. To add to the scandal, Hugh Grant was at the time partnered with British actress and model Liz Hurley, throwing infidelity in with the rest of the tabloid gold.

Hugh had to pay a fine and attend an AIDS education course (a sentence that demonstrates the huge impact that AIDS had on the decade). Meanwhile, Divine Brown was sentenced to more than three months in prison, having violated the conditions of her parole.

Following the incident, Hugh bumbled and mumbled his way through a 'redemption tour' – beginning with an interview with Jay Leno – using his foppish charm to emerge from the scandal with Teflon-like resistance, going on to enjoy a career in film for decades to come. Unsurprisingly, his relationship with Hurley did not last.

Divine Brown capitalised on her newfound fame by making TV appearances, starring in a porn film directed by Ron Jeremy and posing for *Penthouse*. Estimated to have made more than a million dollars following the incident, Divine Brown has since said that she's been able to buy a home and put her children through private school thanks to that fateful moment with Hugh Grant.

O.J. SIMPSON

The mid-90s saw records for network television's highest rating TV shows. But two of the most-watched television moments of that period weren't soap operas or sitcoms, but live-action coverage of a wanted man on the wrong side of the law.

Before 1994, O.J. 'The Juice' Simpson was best known as an NFL Hall of Fame inductee who starred in the *Naked Gun* films. That was until he was implicated in the brutal slaying of his ex-wife, Nicole Brown Simpson and her friend Ron Goldman. When the warrant was issued for his arrest in connection to the murders, America watched in disbelief as O.J. refused to surrender and instead hopped into a vehicle and hit the highway – beginning what is now known as 'The Chase'.

Over the course of two hours, O.J. sat in the back of a white Ford Bronco – having brought with him a gun, his passport, thousands of dollars in cash and a fake goatee and moustache – as police followed and choppers hovered overhead. As one of the first major police chases broadcast live on TV and with such a high-profile fugitive – around 95 million people were gripped.

NBC's coverage of the NBA Finals was interrupted to cover the chase. Bringing new meaning to the term 'domino effect', Domino's Pizza reported a huge sales spike during the car chase, with viewers not wanting to miss a second as the chase unfolded in real time on prime-time TV.

Then, on October 3, 1995, a mind-blowing 150 million Americans (more than half the population of the US) were again glued to the television for O.J.-related content. The verdict's live broadcast was the must-see television event of the year. People watched at home, in lunchrooms, dive bars, and airports. Crowds formed around televisions as people waited for the verdict, and cried (some in sorrow, others in jubilation) when O.J. was declared not guilty.

While the trial's background, history, implications and cultural impact have all been well-reported, the effect the incident had on the way viewers consume crime coverage for entertainment can't be overlooked. O.J.'s case made dissecting criminal cases and trials not just an activity for reporters and legal experts, but a mainstream pastime for ordinary Americans.

THE TRIALS OF
the Menendez Brothers

After Erik and Lyle Menendez were arrested in 1990 for the brutal murder of their parents, the world was captivated by the twists and turns, drama and bizarre characters that emerged during the two gripping trials.

If anything, this case was partly responsible for the popularity of Court TV. Along with the O.J. Simpson case, the 90s saw a huge rise in public interest in criminal proceedings. Court was no longer just a way to determine criminality and dispense justice, but was becoming a legitimate form of entertainment for the masses.

The Menendez Brothers case and trials had everything a true crime buff could want, and more: Two privileged young men accused of shooting their parents to death in their Beverly Hills mansion; an Academy Award–winning 911 phone call made by Lyle; and shocking revelations of child sexual abuse, thought to be fabricated by the brothers to garner sympathy from the jury (this went on to become known as 'the abuse excuse'). Defence attorney Leslie Abramson's eccentric antics and frizzy hairstyle also ensured ratings success for Court TV.

The second trial wasn't televised due to cameras being banned from the courtroom, but the first trial proved to hold most of the explosive material anyway. The two were found guilty and both sentenced to life in prison with no parole. Upon being sentenced, the brothers were separated and sent to different prisons within California where they stayed for nearly thirty years until they were reunited under the same prison roof in 2018.

Like other notable criminals from the decade, the Menendez Brothers' footprints are all over popular culture. The subject of a much-watched Barbara Walters interview in 1996, the siblings were also lampooned in the movie *The Cable Guy* and satirised by *Saturday Night Live* and *In Living Color*.

The Menendez Brothers are now middle-aged, but to a generation of Court TV viewers, they will always be remembered as the clean-cut, sweater-wearing siblings who callously murdered their parents with a 12-gauge shotgun, then went and bought Rolexes and a Porsche to celebrate.

THE BILL CLINTON

& Monica Lewinsky Scandal

From Watergate to the Iran–Contra Affair, presidential scandals are littered throughout the history of the United States. But, there's nothing like a sex scandal to really capture the public's attention.

When news emerged in 1998 that President Bill Clinton had entered into a sexual relationship with a young staffer, political insiders weren't surprised, as Clinton was a known womaniser. What made this scandal so memorable was the extreme level of salacious detail released to the public.

The affair between twenty-two-year-old Lewinsky and forty-nine-year-old President Clinton started in 1995 and lasted for two years. As tawdry details were reported in the media, the world was given rare insight into the sexual behaviour of Clinton, with everyone following 'Zippergate' closely.

Revelations of phone sex sessions between the two, oral sex being performed during official phone calls and a particularly revolting sex act involving a cigar (occurring in the Oval Office no less), no detail was too personal, too revealing or too gross for the media to speculate on.

With Clinton famously declaring that he 'did not have sexual relations with that woman', the President sealed his own fate with a publicly telecast lie that would come back to haunt him when Lewinsky produced her Smoking Gun: a blue dress covered in stains containing Presidential DNA. Once again, no detail was too vulgar for the public to know about.

Clinton was later impeached for lying under oath, but ended up sidestepping most serious consequences to end up serving out the rest of his term before raking in millions for speaking engagements. Post-scandal life was tough for Lewinsky, who struggled with her newfound notoriety and the relentless harassment and public shaming that ensued.

Astoundingly, at the time there was very little discussion of how the affair was a gross abuse of power between the most influential man in America, and a young government employee. In the wake of the #metoo movement, the way the Clinton–Lewinsky Scandal played out shows just how differently incidents like this were viewed and handled in the 90s.

THE Y2K BUG

New Year's Eve, 1999, was a pretty big deal for residents of Planet Earth. The dawning of a new century doesn't happen every day, let alone a new millennium, and was obviously well worth putting on your very best plastic 'Year 2000' novelty sunglasses for. However, celebration can be a little difficult when techno-doomsday is fast approaching.

Also referred to as the Millennium Bug, the Y2K Bug was on everyone's lips in the late 90s. A hypothetical problem (that never eventuated), the Y2K Bug was a supposed coding flaw that would render most of the world's technology obsolete due to 2000 not being recognised as a valid year by computer systems.

All sorts of calamities and catastrophes were predicted to ensue when the world's computer systems simultaneously combusted as the calendar ticked over into the year 2000. Planes would fall from the sky, the stock market would crash, bank accounts would be emptied, nuclear power plants would melt down and public transport systems would grind to a halt.

With some believing that ancient seer Nostradamus foresaw the end of the world in the year 2000, the fearmongering associated with the Y2K Bug accelerated rapidly. It was so strong some doomsday preppers built underground bunkers and stockpiled tinned food, water and weapons to be ready when the shit went down.

In reality, the only shit that went down was a hell of a lot of airplay for Prince's '1999'. The Y2K Bug proved to be bogus and the world lurched on until the 2012 end-of-the-Mayan-calendar panic sparked another wave of doomsday preppers to build apocalypse-proof shelters and start hoarding tinned beans.

INDEX

ACKNOWLEDGEMENTS

Publishing a book requires a *Mighty Ducks*-style team effort, and gosh did I have a great girl-gang working on this book.

Thanks to Hannah Koelmeyer for being the very best editor I know. To paraphrase Mariah Carey, you're the hero that comes along with the strength to carry on.

Big thanks to Lisa Gillard from Meet Me In Shermer for enthusiastically drawing illustrations of everything from Michael Bolton's magnificent mullet to Brenda and Kelly's prom dress debacle.

Cheers also to Stephanie Spartels from Studio Spartels whose design talent made this book look more 90s than the 90s itself.

Proofreaders never get enough credit, so thanks to Pam Dunne for lending me your eagle eye.

Hannah, Steph, Lisa and Pam, we didn't know each other in the 90s but if we did you would all most certainly have been invited over to my place to watch *The Craft* and perform séances in my living room.

Finally, thanks to Paul McNally from Smith Street Books for trusting me with a topic as important as 90s pop culture and giving me free rein to riff on cultural touchstones such as *Showgirls*, Celine Dion film clips and celebrity workout videos.

ABOUT THE

Author

Jo Stewart is an Australian writer who still listens to her Smashing Pumpkins *Siamese Dream* CD bought from Brashs music store in the mid-90s. Her stories about travel, food, people and pop culture have appeared in *Monocle*, *VICE*, *Lonely Planet*, *Women in Pop*, *Mindfood*, *Sydney Morning Herald*, *London Evening Standard* and more.

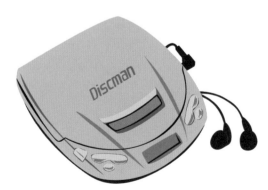

Published in 2019 by Smith Street Books
Melbourne | Australia
smithstreetbooks.com

ISBN: 978-192581102-5
Urban Outfitters ISBN: 978 -192581132-2

The moral right of the author has been asserted.
CIP data is available from the National Library of Australia.

Publisher: Paul McNally
Editor: Hannah Koelmeyer
Design: Stephanie Spartels
Proofreader: Pam Dunne
Illustration: Lisa Gillard, Meet Me In Shermer

Printed & bound in China by C&C Offset Printing Co., Ltd.

Book 85
10 9 8 7 6 5 4 3 2 1